PORTR...

10659133

PORTRAITS OF JESUS

John

A CONTEXTUAL APPROACH
to Bible Study

by
Richard Wortley and William Domeris

COLLINS

Collins Liturgical Publications
8 Grafton Street, London W1X 3LA

Harper & Row
Icehouse One — 401
151 Union Street, San Francisco, CA 94111-1299

Collins Liturgical in Canada
Novalis, Box 9700, Terminal
375 Rideau St, Ottawa, Ontario K1G 4B4

Collins Dove
PO Box 316, Blackburn, Victoria 3130

Collins Liturgical New Zealand
PO Box 1, Auckland

ISBN 0 00 599976 6

Cover illustration by Sidney Holo
Cover design by Malcolm Harvey Young
Typographical design by Colin Reed
Typeset by Swains (Glasgow) Limited
Made and printed in Great Britain
by Collins, Glasgow

Library of Congress Cataloging-in-Publication Data

Wortley, Richard.
  Portraits of Jesus : John.

  1. Jesus Christ—History of doctrines—Early church,
ca. 36—600.   2. Bible. N.T. John—Criticism,
interpretation, etc.   3. Bible. N.T. John—Study.
I. Bible. N.T. John. II. Title.
BT198.W67 1988   266′.506   87—18290
ISBN 0-00-599976-6 (pbk.)

Contents

General Introduction

This study is part of a series of commentaries on the four gospels. The aim of the series is to present the distinct portrait of Jesus which each gospel provides, and yet to do so in a way which shows how the four portraits relate to and complement each other. None of the volumes is therefore intended to be a comprehensive commentary on a particular gospel. The passages chosen for study and reflection have been selected because they portray most vividly the portrait which the evangelist wishes to paint. Yet, when all four volumes are taken as a whole, it will be seen that they cover a great deal of the material found in the four gospels.

The origin of the series is important for understanding what has been attempted. Each of the four authors is a biblical scholar well versed in contemporary discussion on the gospels. In particular, each has a special interest in the sociology of the New Testament and a contextual approach to Christian faith and theology. Even though much scholarly work lies behind each volume, the authors have not sought to engage in scholarly debate. They have provided, rather, commentaries for use in Bible study groups and by people at the 'grass-roots'. Indeed, the commentaries originated as much within such groups as they did within the scholar's study. For several months each author met with various Bible study groups comprised of people from different denominational, racial and socio-economic backgrounds. Together they explored the gospels in order to discern who Jesus really is for us today. Hence the attempt to locate the portrait of Jesus in three contexts or horizons: his own context; the context of the original evangelist and those to whom the gospel was written; and our own situation today. Each of these is pertinent to understanding who Jesus is for us, and they also provide a way into the study of the gospels which has already proved useful in Bible study groups.

The authors have worked as a team, and each of the four volumes follow a similar pattern. All have used the New International Version of the Bible, and, as already indicated, a premium has been placed by all on a sociological approach to the text. Each volume also contains suggestions as to how they can best be used. There is, therefore, a basic structure common to all four volumes. Yet each author has brought to the task different insights and experiences, gained, not least, from discussing the gospels with people who are struggling in different contexts to be faithful to Jesus Christ in South Africa. This, rather than some rigid formula, has shaped the final product. It is our hope that other Bible study groups will find them of value and use for their own journey of faith and obedience within their particular historical and social context. Our overriding concern is that each person discover the Jesus to whom the four evangelists bear witness.

John W. de Gruchy
Bill Domeris
General Editors

This work developed during times of great turbulence and sadness in South Africa.
May truth, understanding and a true quest for justice arise from reflecting on the message of the Bible as it speaks to people in troubled situations everywhere.

Introduction: Framing the Portrait

Three horizons

Open the Gospel of John and you enter into another world. Shut out the buzz of the twentieth century and you will find yourself in a first century realm. There you will wander through the green hills of Galilee, hear your footsteps ring on the cobbled roads of Jerusalem, and stand in awe of the magnificent temple. You will listen to the softly spoken words of Jesus in the upper room. Or tremble at his harsh rebuke aimed at the leaders of the people. In that Palestinian setting you will encounter the first of three horizons to John's portrait of Jesus. The level of the historical Jesus.

The Gospels did not take shape in a vacuum. Each of the four Gospels was shaped by distinctive communities, and each bears the signs of their birth, the scars of their existence. John's Gospel, more than the others, is a mirror of its own socio-political context. The portrait of Jesus which emerges from its pages is not limited to the picture of a Galilean fisherman. The Jesus of John's Gospel is also the Lord of the resurrection community of which John was a member. In the trials and predicaments of this community, we meet the second horizon. The level of the first readers of the Gospel.

The third horizon is the one which we as the readers of the Gospel bring. Each of us reads the Gospel against the backdrop of our own social, political and economic context. Accordingly, the Jesus we encounter is rich or poor, black or white. The power of the Gospel, however, is such that it speaks with equal authority to all our human conditions. The amazing fact about the process of Jesus becoming human is that it identifies Jesus with the joy and pain of all humanity.

The blending of the three horizons occurs so naturally as we read the Gospel, that we sometimes fail to see the richness of the Johannine tapestry. In this series of studies, we shall attempt to draw out the different horizons and, in so doing, make it easier to grasp the relevance of John's picture of Jesus for our own societies. Our first step is to look in more depth at the three horizons.

The first horizon: Palestine

John's Gospel is so different from the other Gospels that some scholars have come to see it as largely the product of the late first century. Yet the Gospel contains much valuable information about the time of Jesus. Geographical notes, place names and political insights which would otherwise have been lost are preserved by John.

We start our study of John with the Palestine of Jesus' time. The land had been shaped by the political and military events of the previous century. The cruel and oppressive rule of the Syrian Seleucids, in the second century BC, had resulted in the most severe persecution of the Jewish religion in the history of the Jews up to that time. Victory was won by the Jewish freedom fighters, the Maccabees, who proudly proclaimed Jewish independence, first religious (164 BC) and then political (142 BC). For the first time in over four hundred years, the Jews enjoyed freedom from foreign domination. They were a nation once more in their own right. They could mint their own coins, make their own foreign policy, and worship God as they chose. A new era began: the age of the Hasmonean priest-kings.

Sadly the golden age was short-lived. Corruption crept into the temple hierarchy. Wealth ousted piety and opulence shackled the hearts of the high priests and their families. Then came the Romans. With their sturdy shields, short stabbing swords and sophisticated military tactics they soon overcame the ragged armies of the Near East. In 63 BC Pompey entered Jerusalem, desecrated the temple and brought an end to Jewish self-rule. So began the era of Jesus' time — Palestine under Roman domination.

Herod the Great in 40 BC became the official ruler of Judaea (including Samaria), Galilee and sections of Trans-Jordan. He was appointed by the Roman senate, and was never accepted by the Jewish people. So he lived his life in constant fear (both real and imagined) of rival claimants to his throne. One after another members of Herod's family died at his hand, several at the instigation of his sister Salome. His murder of his wife marks the climax of this paranoia.

The Temple of Jerusalem was rebuilt by Herod to placate his Jewish subjects. After razing the earlier temple to the ground, Herod enlarged the actual hill by means of a massive retaining wall. The result was a doubling of the temple platform, creating space for a huge, richly decorated, temple area. The lavish expenditure stood in sharp contrast to the poverty which prevailed in the land. The Sadducees (the wealthy priesthood) smiled but the people groaned under the burden of civil and religious taxes. Confused by the propaganda of the time, the people believed that they were serving God.

Like Herod, its creator, the temple was an enigma. It both appealed to Jewish nationalism and was at the same time a symbol of their political oppression. Herod was a Roman puppet, and the mark of his ownership was found above one of the temple gates. There to the utter shame of the Jews who passed beneath it, hung a Roman eagle. Herod was not free to rule as he wished, and the people were not free to decide their own destiny. Even their most sacred act of worship was tainted by the Roman presence. In the days to come, this shame would drive them to open revolt and thousands of Jews would die in the streets of Jerusalem. Daily they prayed for deliverance from their oppressors: 'Look upon our oppression and take our side, and redeem us speedily for your name's sake; for you are a mighty redeemer' (Benediction 7 of the Shemoneh Esreh).

John's Gospel tells us little about the social conditions of Palestine. Part of the reason for this is that he records none of Jesus' parables. Nevertheless, we become aware of two groups of people. These are the leaders (sometimes called 'the Jews') and the common people ('the crowds'). Let us consider each group in turn.

The leaders John mentions the Sanhedrin several times. This was the Jewish parliament and high court. Its membership was drawn from the priestly families and other privileged classes. Its quorum according to the Mishna (the legal code of the time) was only 23. So one can imagine the power of these select few.

We hear in John's Gospel of Pharisees, Sadducees and Scribes as well as the high priest himself. John has a particular concern with the Pharisees, for at the time of writing the Gospel they were the main Jewish group left in existence. The Pharisees were essentially the teachers (of higher education) of Palestine. Unlike the Sadducees who were the great landowners, the Pharisees were largely middle-class. While the Sadducees were pro-Roman, the Pharisees sought a middle path of peaceful co-existence.

On the extreme left were the Sicarii, or dagger men. Their chief concern was the elimination of Roman stooges or sympathisers and, of course, informers. The Zealots, who were similar in outlook to the Sicarii, came into existence as a political party in about 66 AD. This means that they did not exist as a group during the lifetime of Jesus. Moreover scholars suggest that contrary to popular opinion, the group who took refuge at Masada and waged their anti-Roman campaigns in Judaean villages were not Zealots but Sicarii. Josephus, the Jewish historian of that time, calls them bandits. Not only was Josephus pro-Roman, but he was also from the Jewish aristocracy and it is this latter fact which enables us to understand how the rich perceived the Jewish resistance movements: not as freedom fighters, nor Zealots, but as bandits, thugs and murderers.

In John's Gospel, Jesus makes several visits to the Jerusalem temple and indeed the shadow of the temple haunts much of the Gospel. The reason is not difficult to find. The temple was the centre of power for the rulers of the people. Here was where the Sanhedrin met. Here was the place where the peasant farmers paid their tithes and taxes. Here was the store house of the immense wealth of the rulers, the focus of their economic oppression of the people — all in the guise of religious piety and worship.

Annas, whom John mentions, was probably the richest and most powerful person in Judaea. Caiaphas, his son-in-law, was a puppet in his hands. There seems little doubt that it was Annas who masterminded the death of Jesus, because of the exposure Jesus brought to the corruption prevalent amongst those associated with the temple. Jesus' presence in the temple on such a regular basis gives us a sense of the antagonism between the supreme judge Annas and himself. In a sense Jesus is on trial from the beginning of the Gospel when he cleanses the temple (ch 2). The accusations against him punctuate the Gospel record until the moment of the actual trial, when Pilate takes over the position of chief justice.

For John, the presence of Jesus spells the end of the temple. From the moment Jesus sets foot within its walls, it is destined for destruction. The presence of God is no longer in a building of stone, no matter how imposing, but in a person. So the rulers of the Jews represent for John the last remnants of a dying order. A new community has been born.

The people   On Herod's death in 4 BC, his kingdom was divided among his sons. Herod Antipas received Galilee and Peraea (Trans-Jordan), Archelaus received Judaea and Samaria, while Philip received the north eastern section of the kingdom (present day Golan). Of the three, Archelaus had the shortest reign (4 BC-6 AD), and the Romans subsequently took over the active rule of the south. Their first action was a census, the ominous prelude to Roman taxation and the beginning of organized Jewish resistance.

Life in Judaea from this time on was dominated by two factors, Roman oppression and the economic exploitation by the ruling classes (Roman and Jewish). The mass of the people fell into the category either of freed persons (those who had at one time been slaves) or of free persons. Many had started life as peasant farmers struggling to raise cereals in the rocky highlands of the region. But this form of subsistence farming collapsed under the pressure of double taxation, tithes and excessive interest rates. Instead large estates grew up, mainly of olive groves and vineyards. Cereals had to be imported from Galilee and the surrounding regions and so regular food like bread and meal became expensive.

In the place of the community-based economy, in which village industries and communal property ensured the well-being of the inhabitants, the Romans encouraged private ownership. Thus the way was opened for the flourishing of the large estates and the speedy creation of a wealthy class of absentee landlords. Peasants, who had lost their farms because of economic pressures, were forced to rent these same farms and to pay a sizeable percentage of the crop to the owner. This could easily be as much as half the produce. The remainder of the crop went for seed, tithes and rental leaving them very little to live on and little or no profit to safeguard them against famine and misfortune.

Hired labour became the order of the day. People were employed on a daily basis and paid only enough to cover their immediate needs. If no work was forthcoming there would be no food on the table that day. A set of new clothes was a luxury which it might take six months to afford. A bottle of perfume might represent the savings of a lifetime. While the rich enjoyed the good things of life, such as imported wines and spices from the Far East, the poor struggled to buy food. Perhaps without even realizing it, the rich drove the peasants further and further from the lands of their parents. Many peasants were forced to move into the cities, particularly as the Romans introduced cheap slave labour into the rural areas. (The Roman economy was based on slave labour, whereas the Jewish system relied on free villagers working together.)

In their poverty, God seemed far removed. The glory of the temple and the wealth of the ruling classes enhanced this impression. The myth of pious poverty collapsed in the face of increased crime, brutality, sickness and the ever-threatening wave of hopelessness.

Not all the Jews succumbed to that feeling of despair. The people of the *Qumran community*, who wrote several of the Dead Sea scrolls, countered the Roman presence through their creation of an alternative society. All over Judaea and Galilee, little Essene communities sprang up — the Qumran community was just one of many such — dedicated to the preservation of the traditional Jewish system of life. Religious and economic ideals based on Biblical ethics were maintained.

The mark of these Essene communities was their lack of private ownership; all their possessions belonged to the community. Their farming on communal land was devoted to foodstuffs and they produced their own clothing and other necessities of life, like pottery and even their own writing materials. The communities further distanced themselves from the Roman economy by not using slave labour. Each person worked in the fields or at their appointed tasks. So their economy reflected the ideals of the Mosaic law: no taxes, no debts and no poverty.

The Essene communities saw the corruption which took place within the temple walls. At Qumran they actually gave up attending the temple, even for the sacred festivals like Passover and Tabernacles. Instead they spoke of themselves as the new temple. God already dwelt in their midst, just as in the period of the wanderings in the wilderness. They abandoned sacrifices, preferring to speak of their good works as spiritual sacrifices. In an amazing way, many of the features of Christianity were foreshadowed by these religious people. John's Gospel, in particular, comes very close to some of the Essenes' teaching. Whether there was some direct contact between John's Gospel and the Qumran texts, or whether the two communities were structurally similar and so developed similar ideas, is difficult to decide.

The world of Jesus, according to Matthew, Mark and Luke is the world of the Galilean peasantry. In John, it is the world of sectarian Judaism (like Qumran) and the world of Jerusalem. For that reason, we have chosen to leave out a detailed examination of Galilee, (but see the other volumes in this series for an account of Galilean life).

The second horizon: the Johannine community

The Gospel of John is about community life. It arises out of a small group of Christians, living somewhere outside of Palestine, towards the end of the first century AD. Their faith is mirrored in the pages of the Gospel and their triumphant hope in Christ in the face of adversity frames the book. What was the secret of this faith that was able to withstand Roman oppression and Jewish persecution? The answer is simple. The community had experienced an event of the utmost significance: the living presence of Jesus in the person of the Holy Spirit.

The significance of this event is best understood when we realize that the early church faced *two major crises*, which threatened it at its very foundation - its faith in the resurrected Jesus.

The *first* was the death of those people who had known Jesus personally. As these eye-witnesses passed from the scene, the church lost its sense of direct contact with Jesus. The Gospels were in part a response to this need. In the Johannine community it was the death of the beloved disciple which brought a deep sense of loss. The Gospel attempts to compensate for his absence by reminding the Christians of his teachings about Jesus.

The *second* crisis faced by the church was the failure of Jesus to return during the lifetime of those first followers. In John 21:23 we discover that several members of the Johannine community firmly believed that Jesus had promised to return before the death of the beloved disciple. The death of the disciple, without the reappearance of Jesus, came as a shattering blow. John explains that Jesus only suggested he might return then (21:24), but we still sense the pain the community experienced as they wondered how long Jesus would delay.

The Gospel of John responds to the double crisis by appealing to the presence in the community of the Holy Spirit. Who needs a disciple to tell of the historical Jesus, when that same Jesus continues to speak through the Spirit? Jesus did not finish his teaching when he left those first disciples. Instead he promised them that he still had many things to tell them (Jn 16:12), which the Spirit would bring (16:13). John thus opens the door for the Gospel and the Spirit to speak new words to his and our generations. To the question of the continued absence of Jesus, John affirms that Jesus has already returned but *in the person of the Spirit*. In the worship of a Spirit-inspired community, Jesus is present as a living individual.

The author of the Gospel   Tradition has named John, the disciple of Jesus and brother of James as the author of this Gospel. However the Gospel is clearly written by someone other than an eyewitness, since it refers to such a witness for support (Jn 19:35). A middle position is popular among several scholars. This view holds that the beloved disciple was both a disciple of Jesus and the founder of the Johannine community. After his death, someone else wrote the Gospel utilizing the teaching of that disciple as the primary source for the Gospel, but at the same time offering new hope for the grief-stricken community.

For convenience sake we shall refer to the writer of the Gospel as John, and to the founder of the community as the beloved disciple. We shall use the male gender for both.

The location of the Johannine community is unknown. Traditionally John the disciple was resident in Ephesus, but since we do not know for certain that that John is the beloved disciple, such a tradition means very little. The apparent connection between John's Gospel and the Book of Revelation, which is addressed to churches in Asia Minor, is not sufficient grounds for locating the Gospel in the same area. So we are left with almost endless possibilities. One of these is the city of Alexandria in Egypt. It was near here that the oldest fragments of the Gospel were found, and it was here also that Jews and Samaritans argued about the respective merits of their temples at Jerusalem and on Mt Gerezim (cf Jn 4:20).

One may imagine a Christian community living in a cosmopolitan city like Alexandria, surrounded by Jews, Greeks, Samaritans, Romans and other groups. Instead of hiding in the desert like the people of Qumran, they have chosen to follow the example of Jesus and to live out their lives in the world. Bound together by a sense of unity in the face of a hostile world, the community has developed the ideal of equality among its members. Women take positions of leadership and there is a marked absence of the male-dominated hierarchy prevalent in other Christian communities of that time. Indeed one might describe the community as an egalitarian one, based upon Jesus' example of servanthood.

The composition of the community includes both Jews and Gentiles and perhaps even some Samaritans. We know that at this time (towards the end of the first century) there was considerable pressure from the Jewish Council of Jamnia for Jews everywhere to conform to the Pharisaic standards of Judaism. This led to many Jews finding themselves cut off from their roots and considered, by virtue of their beliefs, heretics. A blessing was introduced into the liturgy of the synagogue which was in effect a curse against such heretics. In John 9, we read about excommunication from the synagogue. Probably this chapter reflects the experiences of some of the members of the Johannine community. They have been excommunicated from their synagogues for professing faith in Jesus. Other Christians prefer to be secret disciples of Jesus and so remain in the Jewish fold (Jn 12:42). The fear of the Pharisees keeps them there.

We glimpse a picture of this early community, bonded together by their love for Jesus and for each other, and their common experience of the Holy Spirit. In contrast to the strict Roman hierarchy, they hold to an egalitarian social order. And in contrast to the people of Qumran they live in an urban environment. This was not an escapist group of middle-class charismatics, but a deeply concerned community of Christians, who demonstrated by their life style the practical working out of their faith. For this reason, the Gospel has much to teach us about Christian communal living in the midst of the pressures of modern urban society. In particular, the Gospel mirrors an experience of the Incarnation, when God became a human being and walked among us.

The third horizon: our own context

These Bible studies grew out of a South African context and they unashamedly bear the marks of that birth place. Black and 'coloured' and white Christians met in small groups in the city of Cape Town to struggle with the message of the Gospel of John for South Africa today. The task was a difficult one, and all the tensions and divisions of our society surfaced during our discussions. The State of Emergency hung like a cloud over all our work, a dark pall over our seemingly futile attempts to live out the message of the Incarnation. Police action on the campuses, troops in the townships, detention without trial, torture of detainees, children in jail or re-orientation camps. All these events formed the backdrop against which we read the pages of the Gospel.

You too will bring your own world with you as you read the Gospel. Perhaps the issues you face are different, the problems of your society less obvious. Like us, you will find it difficult to understand the Johannine vocabulary, the code of that early community. But if you use the key of your own personal experience and the issues you face in your community, then the door will open and the riches of the Gospel will pour forth.

The last and most difficult step in the process came when we tried to put into practice the teaching of the Gospel. Time and again we thought of the Incarnation and its meaning for us as Christians. That verse from John's first letter haunted our minds:

> *Dear children, let us not love with words or tongue*
> *but with actions and in truth* (I Jn 3:18).

John's Portrait of Jesus

Jesus, God Made Visible

Imagine a darkened stage with the single focus of a spotlight on one solitary figure. 'In the beginning was the Word.' As the sombre tones of the opening verses of John's Gospel are recited, the figure moves and we recognize Jesus. In amazement, we discover that this person existed before the creation of the world, that all things were made by him (1:3). Jesus is the creator, the giver of life (1:4) and light (1:5). In him truth, grace and glory come together(1:14). He exists in perfect communion with God (1:1), like son and father, like child and parent. Jesus reveals the invisible God (1:18). Indeed Jesus is God (1:1), the only God (1:14).

Halfway through the prologue (vv 1-18) comes the moment of discontinuity, when the Word excellent in its heavenly glory takes on the flesh and blood of humankind (v 14). The stark nature of the contrast breaks the philosophical purity of the opening overture like a grotesque discord, a brutal cacophony. We shiver in amazement that God in divine wisdom saw fit to clothe the Only Child in the garment of our shapelessness.

The drama of the Gospel plays itself out, and other figures enter upon the stage. Like moths to a candle, they are drawn into the presence of Jesus and share for a short time the centre stage. Some stay in its vicinity, while others fade back into the darkness. A Samaritan woman, a blind man, Mary and Martha and the silent Lazarus find faith in their encounter with Jesus. Others find only confusion in the light. Like Nicodemus their minds are cloaked by the darkness of this world. Jesus speaks of new birth and they think of the old, he speaks of the Spirit and they hear the wind. So they return to their comfortable darkness and to the security of their blindness. Judas, Annas, Caiaphas and Pilate are all branded with the sign of disbelief — the stigma of this world. No confession marks their lips and so they cannot take their place with the disciples Nathanael, Peter, Martha and Thomas. The judgement of Jesus pursues them into the darkness.

The Gospel moves from death to life, from judgement to confession. Jesus towers over every scene, dominates every action, even in the Garden of Gethsemane and during the trial and the crucifixion. He is never off-stage. No one moves except in relation to that central figure. By contrast or confession the actors move the drama forward. From the amazed wedding guests of Cana to the homicidal crowds at the trial of Jesus, from the defecting disciples of chapter 6 to the frightened soldiers in Gethsemane, the attention never wavers. The central focus is firm, as slowly but surely John paints his portrait of Jesus. His paintbrush captures the light of Jesus' divinity, the flesh and blood of his humanity, until the work stands complete in all the complexity of its colours and textures. Child of God, Child of Humanity (Son of Man), Holy One of God and Saviour of humankind. Each title brings a dimension of its own, yet can only be appreciated in the light of the whole.

The climax of the Gospel comes with the death of Jesus. Not Paul's moment of deep despair, but the moment of glory. Death and resurrection are one moment in the ascent of Jesus to his Parent God. As the descent of Jesus in the Incarnation occupies the focus of the prologue, so the ascent of Jesus is the theme of the passion. The shame of humanity is destroyed in the wonder of that moment, as Jesus restores the image of God and breaks the bonds of sin. The words of Thomas ring out, 'My Lord and my God', and so the end and beginning come together in the overture to Jesus' divinity.

A note on the choice of texts for study

The confessions mark the steps of faith on the part of the disciples, which culminate in the confession of Thomas. So we have chosen in our first section to focus on the key confessions of faith in an attempt to understand John's portrait of the character and nature of Jesus.

Our second section deals with the theme of life, and is a study of Jesus the giver of life. Here we have chosen passages which deal with Johannine images, like the bread of life and the water of life. The third section is concerned with the reverse side of this image, namely judgement. Jesus comes with life in one hand and judgement in the other. Carefully John preserves this contrast. Nicodemus, a blind man, the Jews and the Jewish leaders are the leading characters in this part of the drama. Finally we end with a look at Jesus' example of servanthood.

We shall return, time and again, to the major theme of John. Jesus reveals the invisible God as he walks the paths of humankind, sharing our joys and sorrows, our pain and oppression. Jesus is the human incarnation of the transcendent deity. He is God's response to the cries of the suffering and oppressed people of our world.

Ways to use this book within a Bible Study

This book is the culmination of the experiences of two very different Bible Study groups. One was a white middle class group and the other a mixed black/white group, from very different parts of Cape Town. To make it easier for readers to follow we decided to merge the two groups experiences into one. So we shall speak about 'the group' or 'the leader' and pool the experiences of both groups and the insights which have added so much to this presentation.

We shall include ideas on the practical implications of the Incarnation which grew out of a black/white group meeting in Johannesburg. We invite you to share our discussions, and to join us in our contextual approach to John's Gospel. From time to time we will suggest that you look at your own social and political context. Take advantage of these occasions and so let the Jesus of John's community speak to you. Then as we did, look for ways in which the message of the Incarnation can take root and grow in your society.

Bible Studies

JESUS, THE MYSTERIOUS PERSON FROM HEAVEN

John's portrait of Jesus, like a flower blooming, takes time to achieve its fullness. The reader follows the steps of the disciples as they struggle with the mystery of Jesus' true identity. Unlike the reader they do not have the prologue to guide them in their search. They do not have the advantage of viewing, as we do, the beginning from the end. They know nothing of the resurrection. Nevertheless, they move ahead slowly and surely towards the confession of Thomas and the climax of the Gospel. Let us the readers now join them in their unravelling of the mystery.

1. The Confession of Nathanael

John 1:43-51

A sense of uncertainty filled the room as we met together for the first time. Not everyone knew each other and some members were sceptical about the direction the studies were to take. The contextual aspect, in particular, caused some of the members concern. Others worried about the critical academic approach of the leaders.

We began with a game, which served both to introduce the new members and the theme of the first study. The object of the game was to guess the occupation of each new member. Twenty questions were allowed, but clues could be given. When we had exhausted the 'unknown' members of the group, the leader spoke about John's method of gradually revealing the identity of Jesus to the reader. The confessions functioned as the major clues, rather than the discourses of Jesus. We then read the passage from John and worked through the notes on the text.

> **43 The next day Jesus decided to leave for Galilee. Finding Philip, he said to him, 'Follow me'.**

[44] Philip, like Andrew and Peter, was from the town of Bethsaida.

[45] Philip found Nathanael and told him, 'We have found the one Moses wrote about in the Law, and about whom the prophets also wrote — Jesus of Nazareth, the son of Joseph.'

[46] 'Nazareth! Can anything good come from there?' Nathanael asked.

'Come and see', said Philip.

[47] When Jesus saw Nathanael approaching, he said of him, 'Here is a true Israelite, in whom there is nothing false.'

[48] 'How do you know me?' Nathanael asked.

Jesus answered, 'I saw you while you were still under the fig tree before Philip called you.'

[49] Then Nathanael declared, 'Rabbi, you are the Son of God; you are the King of Israel.'

[50] Jesus said, 'You believe because I told you I saw you under the fig tree. You shall see greater things than that.'

[51] He then added, 'I tell you the truth, you shall all see heaven open, and the angels of God ascending and descending on the Son of Man.'

Notes on the text

Background

John's story of Jesus begins at 1:19. The majestic chords of the prologue (1:1-18) fade into silence and John the Baptist comes onto the stage. His ministry is located across the river Jordan in the area controlled by Herod Antipas, on the fringe of the desert. A village called Bethany is nearby (not the same Bethany where Mary and Martha live). John's role according to the prologue is to witness to Jesus. Now in vv 19-35, he performs that task. First he distances himself from any claim which might rival those of Jesus. Perhaps when John wrote his Gospel some people were still claiming that John the Baptist was either the Messiah (v 20), a prophet like Elijah (v 21), or a prophet like Moses (v 22). John claims to be nothing more than 'a voice crying in the wilderness' (Isaiah 40:3). So he empties himself to become little more than a foil, a mirror, for the person of Jesus.

The reader suddenly becomes aware that all the time Jesus has been on stage. John the Baptist points to him (vv 26,31). His hearers and followers do not recognize Jesus (v 26) yet he is right in the middle of them. We catch an echo of the Johannine community's struggle to tell the world about the Jesus who stands in their midst.

The confessions made by John the Baptist are the first clues to our mystery. Jesus is the Son of God (v 37), and the Lamb of God (vv 29,35). The meaning of 'Son of God' is not explained. The idea of divinity, however, is not necessarily present. Solomon was a son of God (2 Sam 7:14), as was Adam (Luke 3:38). We may understand the title to be the equivalent of Messiah, at least here in chapter 1.

The Lamb of God (v 29) is explained by reference to the 'bearing away of sin'. We are to understand a pointer here to the death of Jesus, which John interprets as a mighty victory. Therefore the lamb is both a conquering hero and a sacrificial lamb.

The witness of John the Baptist to Jesus ends with the Baptist's disciples beginning to follow Jesus (vv 35-40). While still in this semi-desert region Andrew brings Simon (his brother) to Jesus. He introduces Jesus, not as a prophet but as the Messiah, the royal king (v 41), and so picks up John the Baptist's confession. Simon obviously responds to this view of Jesus and in return receives a new name, Cephas or Peter, meaning a rock. The events recorded in Matthew 16:16-20 occur already at this stage in John's story. The promise of authority, however, will be kept for all the disciples (Jn 20:23 cf Matt 16:19). Peter's role in the Gospel is overshadowed by both the beloved disciple and the community of the disciples as a whole.

Text
John has something greater than the title Messiah in store for Jesus, and so the mystery continues. Jesus now decides to go to Galilee (v 43) and we discover that the disciples are natives of that region. Bethsaida (v 44), meaning 'house of fishing', was on the north shore of the Sea of Galilee. Before Jesus leaves Judaea he asks Philip to follow him. Either while still in Judaea or upon their arrival in Galilee, Nathanael (v 45) hears of Jesus through Philip. Philip introduces Jesus as the one promised in the Law and the Prophets: what we would term the Old Testament or the Hebrew Bible. This can only mean 'the Messiah', the human king who would set the Jews free from their enemies. Son of Joseph was a messianic title like Son of David. John tends to play down the connection between Jesus and David, and so distances Jesus from the Jewish nationalistic hopes. Nevertheless, one can imagine the minds of the disciples buzzing with thoughts of revolution and freedom from the Romans.

Nathanael is not mentioned in the lists of the twelve disciples found in the other Gospels. John appears to be rather critical of the elevation of the Twelve above the many other disciples of Jesus. Here he deliberately raises an unknown disciple above Peter to emphasize the egalitarian nature of the Christian community. It is unlikely that Bartholomew and Nathanael were the same person, as some scholars have suggested.

Nathanael is sceptical of Jesus' lowly origins (v 46) which forces the reader to reflect upon the real origins of Jesus in heaven. 'Come and see', says Philip (v 45), and we can hear the urgency of those tones ringing down through the years. John believed in a Christianity which could be seen!

Nathanael goes to Jesus and is greeted as 'a true Israelite, in whom there is nothing false'. High praise indeed! John uses Israelite not Jew, for the latter term has already acquired a negative sense in his community. 'The Jews' was the term used in the Johannine community for the Jewish leaders of the local synagogue who actively opposed and perhaps even persecuted the community. Moreover, the term Israelite reminds us of v 31 where John the Baptist describes his mission in terms of revealing Jesus to Israel. With the advent of Nathanael that mission is accomplished, for he comes as the representative of all true Israelites, whose minds are purified by faith in Jesus.

The sign of Nathanael's faith, as so often in John, is the confession which he makes. 'Rabbi, you are the Son of God; you are the king of Israel' (v 49). So the true Israelite recognizes the true king of Israel. The latter part of the confession dominates the former, so that Son of God is made subservient to the royal motif. This has the effect of reducing Son of God to the level of a human title, and the whole confession means no more than that Nathanael believes that Jesus is the human king promised in the Old Testament. This belief is consistent with the words of John the Baptist (v 34), Andrew (v 41) and Philip (v 45). But in terms of John's portrait of Jesus it is inadequate.

Instead of Jesus commending Nathanael for his insight, he makes a promise. Nathanael shall see greater things (v 50). Thus Jesus puts a riddle in the path of this eager disciple, one which only a mind trained in rabbinic studies would understand. It appears that 'under the fig tree' was an old expression for describing the rabbinic study of the Hebrew Bible. So Nathanael is challenged to uncover the puzzle of the open heavens and the angels ascending and descending upon the Son of Man (v 51). The reader is also challenged by these words of Jesus, for in v 51 the 'you' is not singular (as in v 50) but plural. All of you, including you the reader, will see this wonderful sign.

What does this riddle mean? The opening statement 'You shall see heaven open' means 'you shall see a revelation about the order of the heavenly realm'. The rest of the riddle refers to two different Rabbinic debates.

1. The first debate was about the dream of Jacob at Bethel (Genesis 28:10-17). The Hebrew text has a curious difficulty, which the rabbis with their scrupulous attention to detail had noticed. Did the angels ascend or descend upon the ladder or upon Jacob? The Hebrew could be read either way.

2. The second debate arises out of the rabbinic study of Daniel 7 and the mention of 'thrones' in v 9. God obviously occupied only one throne, so to whom did the other thrones belong? Since the other figure in the vision is the angelic one like a Son of Man (that is, like a human being), he is a possibility. Such a debate led to the belief in more than one power in heaven. The debate was consequently not encouraged in Rabbinic circles, but nevertheless it continued throughout the New Testament and long afterwards.

John uses the two debates to introduce two clues, which those familiar with the debates would readily pick up. The first is the hint of Jesus as the mediator between God and humanity. The second is the connection which he will develop between the title Son of Man (Child of Humanity) and the divinity of Jesus. The writer will use the title to counter the purely human overtones of Messiah.

The moment of this supreme revelation is obviously the death of Jesus. There at the cross one person in particular receives a special revelation (Jn 19:35) and is so able to testify to the actual death of Jesus. Was that person Nathanael or the Beloved Disciple? Or are they one and the same?

Discussion

The group spent some time speaking about the different titles for Jesus encountered in this chapter. Several members were quite surprised to discover that the term Messiah did not automatically imply Jesus' divinity. As we thought about John's use of titles, we realized that John did not reject the title Messiah, but by linking it with the title Son of Man, gave it a new Christian content. As all titles change their meaning depending on the person to whom they are applied (eg President), so the titles applied to Jesus underwent similar changes. Messiah lost its nationalistic overtones and developed a cosmic dimension. Since John was writing after the abortive revolution in Palestine (66-70 AD), he knew that Jewish nationalism had suffered a terrible blow. It was therefore important to distance Jesus from the failure of that movement.

The question was then raised of the validity of connecting Jesus with a particular nationalistic movement. Could God be said to be on one side of a political struggle? Our own reading of the Old Testament suggested that the answer was 'yes'. We then looked at our own socio-political struggles using the following reflection as an introduction. The debate which followed was a lively one.

Reflection

The cold seeping rain of that Cape winter morning created a world of mist and half-glimpsed figures. Clustered around the fires they stood, struggling to keep warm. The wind carried the low murmur of voices and the hacking coughs of the children to the silent men in uniform. Then the order was given and the diesel engines coughed into life. The bulldozers moved forward like savage giants trampling all in their path. With a cry the people launched themselves forward in an attempt to save their material possessions. Pitifully they clung to the odd chair, a mirror or a cardboard box. Finally silence descended and the people moved back to their fires singing, 'My God, my God why have you forsaken me?'

A few kilometres away in a luxurious home, a white child slept in warmth and comfort. On the wall hung a picture of Jesus with the words 'God answers prayers'.

Whose prayers does God answer?

2. The Confession of Peter

John 6:60-71

Our group commenced the second study by reading the reflection below and then used it as a basis for a time of discussion. The result was a very interesting debate on the role of the church in society today. Two issues emerged. The first was the extent to which a local church could take a united stand on a political or social issue. The second was the more basic issue of 'politics in the pulpit'. Our group had clearly different views on these issues, particularly on the idea of the church taking sides.

Reflection

A shaft of sunlight filtered through the multi-coloured lights of the stained glass window. It softened the stones of the little church which stood so proud and strong. In the sanctimonious gloom the Christians sat. Joyous refrains and intelligent prayers filled the air. Thoughts focused superficially inwards, and minds filtered the words of the sermon, selectively hearing the words of comfort and assurance. The central heating gave everyone a sense of well-being. 'If God be for us, who can be against us?' they murmured happily.

Sitting in church, smugly complacent.
While the world rushes by,
with a sickening cry.
Deaf to those sounds
which remind us of suffering.
Dumb to those calls
for costly discipleship.
Paralysed by our commitment
to inactivity.
Praising the god
of our silent apathy.

[60] On hearing it many of his disciples said, 'This is a hard teaching. Who can accept it?'

[61] Aware that his disciples were grumbling about this, Jesus said to them, 'Does this offend you?

[62] What if you see the Son of Man ascend to where he was before!

[63] The Spirit gives life; the flesh counts for nothing. The words I have spoken to you are spirit and they are life.

[64] Yet there are some of you who do not believe.' For Jesus had known from the beginning which of them did not believe and who would betray him.

[65] He went on to say, 'This is why I told you that no one can come to me unless the Father has enabled him.'

⁶⁶ From this time many of his disciples turned back and no longer followed him.

⁶⁷ 'Do you want to leave too?' Jesus asked the Twelve.

⁶⁸ Simon Peter answered him, 'Lord, to whom shall we go? You have the words of eternal life.

⁶⁹ We believe and know that you are the Holy One of God.'

⁷⁰ Then Jesus replied, 'Have I not chosen you, the Twelve? Yet one of you is a devil!'

⁷¹ (He meant Judas, the son of Simon Iscariot, who, though one of the Twelve, was later to betray him.)

Notes on the text

Background

After the confession of Nathanael, the Gospel takes us through a series of signs which Jesus performs. These are not just miracles, for John intends a deeper meaning for each of them, whether it is the water into wine or the feeding of the 5000. Each sign has something to add to John's portrait of Jesus, for each of the signs points beyond the fact of the miracle to the person of the worker of miracles — that is to Jesus.

In spite of these miracles, there is no great turning to faith. Indeed, we are warned of the dangers of a faith which rests upon the miraculous (Jn 2:23-5), especially when that faith caters to our physical needs. Such faith can only be shallow and insincere and ultimately blind. Jesus takes the people to task on this very issue (Jn 6:26). Their motives for following him are selfish, and they cannot see beyond the miracle and so find faith in Jesus.

Jesus' lengthy sermon in chapter 6 takes the reader from the miracle of the feeding into the issues which face Christians of all generations, but particularly those which face the Johannine community. The questions (vv 28, 34, 42 and 52) echo the questions of the people that the community is trying to win to faith in Jesus. The same point is made again and again. As Moses gave the people manna to eat in the desert, God gives Jesus to the world. He is the true Bread of Life, and those who share the fellowship of his table will live forever (vv 53-57). So John takes us from the hills of Galilee into the experience of the risen Jesus in the celebration of the eucharist. There we and the original readers are united in our common experience with those first disciples who shared food with Jesus.

Text

The onset of a crisis looms within the ranks of the disciples (v 60). Once again we are aware that the history of Jesus and that of the Johannine community overlap. Indeed that crisis refers to an event both in the life of Jesus and in the life of the community. In this way, John uses the teaching of Jesus to encourage his church as it strives to understand what is happening to it, and why some people have left the community to go their own way (1 Jn 2:19).

Jesus asks his disciples whether they are shocked (*lit.* scandalized) by his teaching. We are reminded of Paul's words on the offensiveness of the Christian faith (1 Cor 1:23). As in Corinth, so here in Galilee, that offensiveness proves to be a stumbling block for some of the disciples and they will turn away from Jesus.

In v 62 Jesus introduces again the mysterious 'Child of Humanity' (Son of Man) title. 'If you were to see me return to heaven, would you believe that I came from heaven?' is the gist of his question. Here is another clue for the reader, reminding us of that figure in John 1:51 (cf Jn 3:13).

In the next verse, Jesus utters a warning. Neither the elements of communion, nor of any other sacrament, is effective in itself as an agent of salvation. Some Christians in the early second century believed that the eucharist was a kind of 'life-giving' drug. John has Jesus counter this belief. Salvation comes only through the words of Jesus and the Spirit which he brings.

Jesus refers to the unbelief of some of the hearers (v 64). Remember these are not the crowds, but his own disciples. We realize from John's Gospel that Jesus had far more than just twelve disciples. Not all of them remain faithful to the end. Jesus' ability to read the hearts of his followers marks him out as superhuman. It also reassures John's first readers that Jesus, at least, was not surprised when some of the community left (cf 1 John 2:19).

The supernatural gift of faith is emphasized in v 65. God gives faith to people in exchange for their sincere acceptance of Jesus. This is neither predestination nor election, but the mystery of 'God's enabling'. In his own experience, John knows that some people are receptive to the message of the Gospel and others are not, that some people hold on to their faith and that others lose it. He does not pursue the mystery.

The moment of actual crisis comes in v 66. Many of Jesus' disciples turn back and no longer follow him. At the secondary level, of John's community, this is the split in the community referred to in 1 John 2:19.

> They went out from us, but they did not really belong to us. For if they had belonged to us, they would have remained with us; but their going showed that none of them belonged to us.

Why did these people leave the community? It appears that they denied that Jesus was the Messiah (1 Jn 2:22) and were trying to lead the rest of the Christians astray (1 Jn 2:26). Perhaps these are the same 'secret disciples' who refused to risk confessing Jesus as Messiah, in order to remain part of the synagogue community (cf Jn 12:42f).

In the face of the 'many' who desert him, Jesus now turns to the 'few'. 'Do you want to leave too?' he asks (v 67). The Greek form of the question implies that Jesus expected them to say 'no'. Peter, as the leader of the twelve, then responds with a confession of faith.

'Lord, to whom shall we go?' The plural 'we' indicates that Peter speaks on behalf of others. Indeed he is the representative not only of the twelve, but of all faithful disciples including the faithful few in the Johannine community. Jesus is the bearer of the words which bring eternal life — the message of salvation. To the saviour of the world, Peter responds.

'We believe and know [have come to know]' (v 69). Beyond belief is the knowledge derived from experience of Jesus. Peter speaks out of his experience of Jesus, and John writes out of his relationship with his resurrected Lord. Instinctively the reader is drawn towards an appreciation of this faith. A desire grows to take that faith and make it her/his own.

'The Holy One of God' (v 69) is not an easy title to understand. That is why so many of the early manuscripts altered the title to read 'Messiah' or 'Son of God' instead. Thus the confession of Peter in John was made the same as in Matthew 16:16, or Mark 8:29. But John has something else in mind. The ancient Hebrew idea of a holy one was that of an agent, perhaps even a heavenly agent who represents God on earth. The reader knows that Jesus is in fact God's heavenly agent, although Peter, at this stage, does not understand this dimension. Nevertheless, Peter so far is the closest anyone has come to an appreciation of Jesus' special nature in the Gospel. From this time on, the confessions will move from the mission of Jesus (as Messiah or, as here, Agent or Holy One) to his person and in particular his divinity. Peter's confession prepares the way for that ultimate step.

In the last two verses (vv 70-71), the focus is on Judas. An important contrast occurs here which reminds us of Mark (1:23-26), in which a demon-possessed man calls Jesus the Holy One of God. In both stories, Jesus the Holy One is contrasted with evil. A terrible collision of forces occur, with Jesus representing the power and might of God opposing the forces of evil. Here in John, the power of evil is represented by Judas. So the reader is left with the sense of the crisis which the presence of Jesus creates, forcing apart good and evil, and exposing that evil in all its ugliness. Both in his own time and in the present!

Discussion

We spent some time working through the implications of confessing Jesus today. We referred from our own experiences to situations where confessing the truth had divided communities. So often the truth is hard to hear and those who speak it are branded trouble makers, revolutionaries and communists. We thought of people in our own community who had dared to speak the truth in spite of its unpopularity. Some of those people had lost their jobs. In one case a Methodist minister had had his house petrol-bombed because he spoke out against the State and its puppets. Are there people in your community who have been branded for their stand against evil? What are Christians doing about the problem?

Some members of the group were against the idea of Christians becoming politically involved in the present struggle. Christians should pray and preach, but not become actively involved. This created a split in the group, for other members believed that political involvement was essential for all Christians. So we became aware that the words of Jesus still cause division. Yet we needed to listen to each other and together find out what God was saying to us today. Only then would we be able to confess Jesus and to share in the suffering of his fellowship. Think about your own community. What do you think God is saying to you today about the socio-political issues you face? Has you church taken sides in the struggle against evil? Or is it still on the fence?

3. The Confession of Martha

John 11:17-27

The evening started with a number of short sketches dealing with the typical stereotypes of women which one encounters in our societies. These were humorous, but somewhat painful to watch for several of the men in the group. We then spoke about the oppression of women, which led to a discussion on structural violence (meaning that form of violence which attacks a person's self-esteem). One student spoke about the rape of womanhood perpetrated by the advertising media. She meant, of course, the degrading of women to the level of sexual stimuli to promote sales. This caused no little debate and it was some time before we came to read the notes and the Biblical text.

17 On his arrival, Jesus found that Lazarus had already been in the tomb for four days.
18 Bethany was less than two miles from Jerusalem,
19 and many Jews had come to Martha and Mary to comfort them in the loss of their brother.
20 When Martha heard that Jesus was coming, she went out to meet him, but Mary stayed at home.
21 'Lord,' Martha said to Jesus, 'if you had been here, my brother would not have died.
22 But I know that even now God will give you whatever you ask.'
23 Jesus said to her, 'Your brother will rise again.'
24 Martha answered, 'I know he will rise again in the resurrection at the last day.'
25 Jesus said to her, 'I am the resurrection and the life. He who believes in me will live, even though he dies;
26 and whoever lives and believes in me will never die. Do you believe this?'
27 'Yes, Lord,' she told him, 'I believe that you are the Christ, the Son of God, who was to come into the world.'

Notes on the text

Background

After the confession of Peter, John takes the reader into the thick of the rising conflict between Jesus and the Pharisees. With the ominous blackness of an African thunderstorm, the moment of the final showdown comes near. The last straw for the Pharisees is the raising of Lazarus (ch 11). In Mark and the other Gospels, it was the cleansing of the temple which led to the final decision to execute Jesus. But there the focus was upon the Sadducees and their corrupt rule over the economy of Judaea. Here in John, the crunch is the raising of a dead man.

For fear that many will believe and follow Jesus and that this will lead to revolution and Roman action, the Pharisees now join forces with the Chief Priests (Sadducees) in a meeting of the Sanhedrin (Jn 11:47-53). They argue that Jesus will cause them to lose their temple and their nation (11:48). The reader knows that in fact it was Jewish nationalism and Sadducean corruption which led to the Roman destruction of Jerusalem in 70 AD. The logic is false and this alerts the reader to the true issue at stake — the power struggle which exists between the Jewish leaders and Jesus: this is the real reason for his death. The raising of Lazarus, who was well-known to the Pharisees (11:46), threatens their authority. One man must die to save the nation (v 50) or, more correctly, to save their personal power. So they plot Jesus' death.

What was it about the death of Lazarus that is so threatening? For the benefit of the reader, John spells out the significance of the miracle in advance (11:23-27) in a fascinating dialogue between Jesus and Martha, the sister of Lazarus. At the same time he opens the way for the penultimate confession of faith in the Gospel — and that from a woman! In this way, John gives us a glimpse of the unusual status women enjoy in his community.

Text
Jesus arrives in Bethany (close to Jerusalem and so different from the Bethany of ch 1). This is the home town of three of Jesus' friends Mary, Martha and Lazarus. The sisters are also mentioned in Luke (10:38-41). In both Gospels they appear to be women of independent means and apparently either unmarried or widowed, since there is no mention of their husbands. Luke presents Mary as the listener, and Martha as the worker. John turns the pattern around. Mary stays at home, and Martha makes the confession of faith (ch 11). Then in John 12, the pattern resembles Luke's picture. Mary anoints Jesus's feet while Martha serves and Lazarus reclines as host.

Lazarus has been dead for four days (v 17), which means that by this stage he is well and truly buried. Martha leaves the mourners to go and meet Jesus. She greets him as 'Lord', which hints at Jesus' true identity and marks a contrast with other titles like 'Rabbi' or 'Teacher'. This is a clue for the reader, rather than an indication of Martha's insight (cf v 28).

The dialogue which follows, like the conversations with the Samaritan woman and Nicodemus, uses misunderstanding as a means of teaching the reader a spiritual truth about Jesus. Here Martha will misunderstand the meaning of resurrection, so that Jesus can explain the already present reality of resurrection life. What the Johannine community experienced as a daily occurrence — the presence of the eternal Christ — is contrasted with the traditional Jewish belief in life after death. Yet the dialogue is more than just a lesson in doctrine. It is a real conversation between an angry and heart-broken woman and Jesus. 'Where were you when I needed you?' is the gist of her comment in v 21. Her voice is filled with accusation. Then in hope she begs Jesus to do something, anything, for God listens to him (v 22). Desperation fills her voice.

'Your brother will rise again' is Jesus' simple statement of fact. Martha interprets this in line with the traditional Jewish expectation of the Pharisees. 'At the last day' is her half question, half statement (v 24). Then comes the contrast as Jesus reveals to her that where he is death cannot stay (vv 25f). Those who believe in him will enjoy a unique relationship with him. *That relationship will never die.* Only from a context like the Johannine community could such a statement of faith ring so true. They knew that Jesus was in their midst, and that not even death could separate them from Jesus.

'Do you believe?' asks Jesus. 'Yes, Lord' responds Martha and we hear her deep confession of faith in Jesus as more than just the Messiah, but as the very Son of God and the one who comes into the world. So the confession of faith in John's Gospel includes that of Nathanael (King), of Peter (the agent of God), and of John the Baptist (Son of God). But the order, from less to greater, shows us that the combination is much more than just the sum of the three. Jesus is the Messiah, but he is also the divine Son of God, who comes from heaven. This is the full gist of the confession and measures up to the standard John sets for true belief (20:31):

> But these are written that you may believe that Jesus is the Christ, the Son of God, and that by believing you may have life in His name.

The confession of Martha is the most important clue to the identity of Jesus up to this point. Here the divinity of Jesus is laid bare for all to see. But one senses that Martha does not yet understand the full significance of her words. The disciples have still to encounter the risen Jesus before they can arrive at the true knowledge of Jesus. Nevertheless an important bridge has been crossed. Martha is the symbol of the female disciples of Jesus, who as members of John's community stand side by side with the men. In the community of Christ, there is no dividing line between the sexes. The Holy Spirit inspires with equal zeal both men and women, and divine truth is not the property of one or the other.

Even as John wrote his Gospel, the basic elements of a male-only priesthood were being established in Asia Minor. The hierarchy of deacons, elders and bishops was deemed to be mirrored in the heavenly hierarchy of God, Jesus and the twelve apostles. The partnership between the sexes known to Paul (Rom 16:12) is replaced by a sexist view that only men were created in the image of God and so able to represent 'Him'. The freedom of the Spirit and the free use of the charismata (gifts), is destroyed by the institution of the male only priesthood.

Martha's confession cries out against the oppression of women and the denial of their rights before God. It affirms once and for all the right of women to be full disciples of Jesus and the bearers of divine revelation. It refutes those who would silence women in churches. In the face of male hierarchies, the Johannine community, through its Lord, affirmed the right of women to be the spiritual leaders and teachers of their community.

Discussion

We steered the debate away from a discussion of those churches which discriminate against women, towards a more practical level. What could we do to affirm the right of women? We started with the women in our group. It was interesting to see how some women were conscious of discrimination, while others, tired of fighting it, had reached a stage of passive acceptance. Amongst the men, there was a definite resistance to the changing of the present social norms. Nevertheless as a group we came to see that there would be no real freedom in the new South Africa (Azania), unless that included the freedom of women. A very definite change in the current treatment of women was needed.

In the light of John's presentation of Martha, we began to see that equality between the sexes was as much a Christian issue as the fight against Apartheid or any other form of discrimination. Moreover it carries the stamp of Jesus' own practice.

Reflection

He spoke of freedom and dreamed of the day when his people would be free. He sang the freedom songs and joined a banned organization. He encouraged the people of his block to work together for justice and truth, for liberty, equality and fraternity. Twice arrested, he remained unafraid for he was prepared to die for his cause.

She too thought of freedom as she washed the dishes, cleaned the house, bathed and dressed the children. She sang her freedom songs as she rose before dawn to feed her family, before she joined the busy throng that rushed towards the city. In the hospital, she encouraged the other nurses with the words she had heard the leaders say. And all the time she prayed for the day when her husband would recognize that he was no less an oppressor and she doubly oppressed.

There is No Freedom Until Women are Also Free.

4. The Confession of Thomas
John 20:24-29

A sense of commitment to the other members of the group was noticeable the next time the group met. To reinforce this mood, we decided to spend time in pairs talking to each other about 'something on my mind'. After ten or fifteen minutes, each prayed for the other person in the pair, either aloud or silently. As a small group we had begun to grow and to experience something of what the Johannine community had discovered. Later, as we spent more time together, this understanding would deepen.

²⁴ **Now Thomas (called Didymus), one of the Twelve, was not with the disciples when Jesus came.**
²⁵ **When the other disciples told him that they had seen the Lord, he declared, 'Unless I see the nail marks in his hands and put my**

finger where the nails were, and put my hand into his side, I will not believe it.'

[26] A week later his disciples were in the house again, and Thomas was with them. Though the doors were locked, Jesus came and stood among them, and said, 'Peace be with you!'

[27] Then he said to Thomas, 'Put your finger here; see my hands. Reach out your hand and put it into my side. Stop doubting and believe.'

[28] Thomas answered, 'My Lord and my God!'

[29] The Jesus told him, 'Because you have seen me, you have believed; blessed are those who have not seen and yet have believed.'

Notes on the text

Background

John's story of Jesus moves inexorably towards its conclusion. Nearly half the Gospel is devoted to the last week of Jesus' life, so one soon realizes the immense importance of the events which took place during those few days. After the crisis of the death of Lazarus, the plotting of the Pharisees moves swiftly to its culmination. The spectre of the cross looms large and even the anointing of Jesus by Mary anticipates that moment (Jn 12:7). While the reader prepares her/himself for the final show down between Jesus and his enemies, s/he knows it is also the moment of supreme revelation (Jn 1:51 and 8:28).

The crucifixion account is dominated by the power of Jesus, even here at the moment of his apparent weakness. No one takes Jesus' life from him (Jn 10:18). In fact John reverses the normal Greek phrase when he describes Jesus' death (19:30). Jesus voluntarily gives up his spirit, rather than the spirit leaving him.

After the death of Jesus, the resurrection account follows. Two traditions meet in chs 20 and 21 of John's Gospel: the tradition that Jesus appeared to his disciples first in Jerusalem (following Luke), and the second tradition that he appeared to them in Galilee (Mark and Matthew). They stand quite happily side by side here in John.

Chapter 20 opens with the familiar story of the garden and the women. In this case it is one woman, Mary of Magdala, not the prostitute of popular imagery, but a person whom Jesus had healed (Lk 8:2) and who became a loyal disciple of the Lord. She finds the empty grave (v 1) and tells Peter and the beloved disciple. Peter sees the empty grave, but the beloved disciple 'believes' (v 8). John contrasts Peter and the beloved disciple three times in the Gospel (at the Last Supper, here and in ch 21). Each time the beloved disciple appears to advantage. Thus John emphasizes the importance of faith over status, and the basic equality of all people before God.

A moving scene between Jesus and Mary follows (vv 10-18). Alone of the four Gospels, John has Jesus appear first of all to a woman. Again the importance of women in the Johannine community comes to the fore. After this Jesus appears to the other disciples. We are not to think just of the eleven, for John does not limit the term 'disciples' just to that group. All these disciples, men and women, receive the Holy Spirit directly from Jesus (20:22), thus forming a direct bond between Jesus and the disciples.

The Gospel reaches out to its climax, and to the fulfilment of the promise of the revelation which Jesus' death brings. The person chosen for the final confession is a little-known disciple named Thomas. Only here in John does he receive some attention. Typical of John is his tendency to name the disciples and to attribute questions to them individually. In the other Gospels only Peter is singled out in this way. Thomas is a brave follower prepared to die for Jesus. When the disciples are afraid to go with Jesus back to Jerusalem, it is Thomas who encourages the others: 'Let us also go, that we may die with him' (Jn 11:16). Later it is Thomas who asks where Jesus is going (Jn 14:5) and in reply is told that if he really knew Jesus, he would know God also (Jn 14:7). This word is in fact a promise to Thomas and indirectly to the Christian believers.

Text

The words of Thomas (v 25) stress the personal (note the 'I') as well as the experiential (see, put my finger, put my hand). Thomas recognizes the incredible nature of the resurrection. His request is not a token of his lack of faith, but a realistic appraisal of the claim that a person can rise from the dead. Our scientific culture readily understands his predicament.

The wonderful fact about this story is that Jesus both understands Thomas' cry and responds to it. Jesus meets Thomas at the point of his need (v 27). In his crisis of faith, Jesus comes to restore faith. No rebuke is necessary, just his presence. Thomas is told to stop doubting (now) and believe (v 27), and he does. The wounds of Jesus speak to Thomas about a love that was so great that it drove Jesus to die for his friends (Jn 15:13). These wounds are the mute testimony to Jesus' caring.

Thomas responds to this love and to the whole event of the resurrection. His confession (v 28) reflects the depth of John's understanding of Jesus, and is the crowning glory of his portrait. The revelation sees beyond the resurrected Jesus, and Thomas apprehends the divinity of Jesus. 'My Lord and my God' brings to mind the words of the prologue — 'In the beginning was the Word (Jesus) and the Word was God' (1:1f). So the climax of the Gospel found here in the confession of Thomas and the opening words of the prologue join together in a single theme. Jesus and God are one.

Jesus speaks to Thomas (v 29) and indirectly to all Christians. Thomas believes because he has seen, and is blessed for his faith. But how much more blessed (happy) are those who have not seen Jesus (the Johannine community included) and yet who believe. The experience of the presence of Jesus in Spirit is the living assurance for those early Christians of Jesus' presence. They may not be able to see him, but they can sense that he is there.

One crisis faced by the Johannine community was the death of the beloved disciple before Jesus returned (Jn 21:22f). Remember that many early Christians believed that Jesus would return in the glory of the Kingdom of God before the death of the very first disciples. The story of Thomas reassures the reader. Jesus did appear and that was in physical form. One day he will come back again in the same way, but for the moment the experience of Thomas is enough. All Christians everywhere can share in that moment of joy and know in a spiritual way that same encounter with the risen Lord. So John takes the faith of the community beyond the moment of crisis.

Discussion

We used the reflection to focus on the fact of Jesus showing Thomas his wounds. We likened this to Christians today who bear the scars of their faith. We mentioned some names, and you might like to make up your own list. We tried to decide what it was that made ordinary women and men into such important examples of Christian living.

Then we went on to a discussion of some of the ordinary ways in which Christians are called upon to suffer.

One of the topics which came up was Religious Objection. Young men who refuse to fight in the South African Defence Force are allowed to appeal on religious grounds. If their appeal is successful they are granted alternative service in a non-military capacity. The duration of this service is one and a half times the normal length of military service, done without a break. So most of these young men face six years continuous service, instead of two years and several four month camps. Their pay is a pittance, and often the work is well below their academic level, eg a nuclear scientist worked as a filing clerk. Sadly many of the Christians who went this path found themselves rejected by friends, family and other Christians.

Perhaps there are people in your community who suffer because of their Christian convictions. What can you do to support them?

Reflection
Social concern was the slogan of his life. He wore it on the badges of his faded duffle coat, and around the crown of his battered felt hat. A student of politics with a degree in economics, and a Christian to boot. His nights were filled with long earnest conversations about the evil of society or intellectual debates with less enlightened acquaintances. Left of centre, a socialist by persuasion: that summed him up. Change was his concern, not reform but complete change. Yet for all his sincerity, he never seemed to win the friendship of the people he tried so hard to help. They treated him no differently to their oppressors. One day in desperation he cried out, 'What must I do to show you that I really care, that I am different?'

'Show us your scars' was their reply.

JESUS, THE LIFE GIVER

Having traced the development of John's portrait of Jesus from one confession to the next, we are now ready to explore one of the major themes in John, namely Jesus as the giver of life. Life for John transcends both the confines of the present and the expectations of the future. Thus John breaks through the categories which separate the present from the future. Already here on earth we taste eternal life. Indeed by the mere fact that we believe in Jesus, we possess eternal life and have passed from judgement into life (Jn 5:24). Like people held hostage and fearing for their lives, we are suddenly free and the threat of death evaporates into the fresh air.

John uses several images for life, all deriving from the basic necessities of life. Water (ch 4), bread (ch 6) and light (ch 8). As a prelude to this theme, John invites us to join him at a wedding in Cana, where Jesus is present. For at this wedding we will have a taste of the life which Jesus brings, and the joy which he shares with his friends.

5. The Wedding

John 2:1-11

We began our study with one of our members telling us, in great detail, about an African wedding. Little did we know how similar to weddings of Jesus' time it would turn out to be. This led to a general discussion on weddings and of the things which can and do go wrong. In particular we realized that just one guest could either spoil a wedding or conversely make it very special.

¹ On the third day a wedding took place at Cana in Galilee. Jesus' mother was there,

² and Jesus and his disciples had also been invited to the wedding.

³ When the wine was gone, Jesus' mother said to him, 'They have no more wine.'

⁴ 'Why do you involve me?' Jesus replied, 'My time has not yet come.'

⁵ 'His mother said to the servants, 'Do whatever he tells you.'

⁶ Nearby stood six stone water jars, the kind used by the Jews for ceremonial washing, each holding from seventeen to twenty-five gallons.

⁷ Jesus said to the servants, 'Fill the jars with water'; so they filled them to the brim.

⁸ Then he told them, 'Now draw some out and take it to the master of the banquet.' They did so,

⁹ and the master of the banquet tasted the water that had been turned into wine. He did not realize where it had come from, though the servants who had drawn the water knew. Then he called the bridegroom aside.

[10] and said, 'Everyone brings out the choice wine first and then the cheaper wine after the guests have had too much to drink; but you have saved the best till now.'

[11] This, the first of his miraculous signs, Jesus performed in Cana of Galilee. He thus revealed his glory, and his disciples put their faith in him.

Notes on the text

Background

Weddings during the time of Jesus took place in two stages. In the first stage, a contract was drawn up between the bride and groom in the presence of the two families, who acted as the witnesses. From that moment the couple were considered to be married. They were called husband and wife and could only separate by means of a divorce certificate. However, they did not live together, but stayed on for up to a year in the homes of their respective parents.

The second stage occurred at the end of this time, on a date agreed upon by the parents. On the wedding day, the bride processed in all her finery to the home of her husband. She made herself and her bridesmaids comfortable and settled down to wait for the bridegroom. He meanwhile was at the equivalent of his bachelor party. The celebrations began around midnight, when the bridegroom made his, not too steady, way back to his home. He was met near his house by the bridesmaids who hurried him into the main room of the house to meet the bride. Then the guests retired into the courtyards and noisily celebrated through the night and through the following days, stopping only to catch up on their sleep. The bride and groom emerged periodically from the house to join the celebrations.

At the wedding in Cana, we encounter the second stage of the marriage, with the guests celebrating at the home of the groom. The festivities are in the hands of the best man, here referred to as 'the master of the banquet'. Due to the length of the celebrations, the master had to decide on the most judicious time to bring out the next pithos (jar) of wine, purchased in advance by the groom. As the custom was to water down the wines, it was also his task to decide upon the correct quantities. A strong wine (in Hebrew a 'sleeping wine'), often imported from the Greek islands, might be watered down to one part wine and twenty parts water.

Text

Our story unfolds. As usual John alerts the reader to the time and place. It is the third day (presumably after Jesus' arrival in Galilee), and the place is a very small village called Cana (v 1). Mary, the mother of Jesus and a key character in the Gospel is present and we learn that Jesus and his new friends have been invited (v 2). Perhaps they are house guests of Jesus, and so were automatically invited along with Mary, the head of the house.

The wine is soon exhausted (v 3). Given the pressures facing the peasants of Galilee in the form of heavy taxation, tithes and expensive food costs, this was not an uncommon occurrence. Few peasants could afford to supply wine for as long as custom dictated. Moreover the poorer the wine, the less water could be added to it. Most of the imported wine in Jerusalem was consumed by the wealthy land owners.

Jesus' mother tells him about the wine. Perhaps she feels guilty because of all Jesus' friends who are with them. Jesus responds with the rather formal address, 'Woman, . . . the time (of my death) has not yet come' (v 4). Jesus means that it is not yet time for his blood to be poured out. The allusion to the eucharist is unmistakable. Meanwhile Mary, who knows her son well enough to ignore his outbursts, warns the servants to obey his instructions. We note the authority which Mary carries.

Six stone water jars (v 6) stand nearby, holding a total of 600 litres or 180 gallons (US). This is a huge quantity of water, well in excess of the normal requirements for a household. Either the main source of water in the area was a long way away, or the household were as fanatical about washing as the Essenes. Josephus (a Jewish historian of the first century AD) records that they used to bathe every day. Highly unusual in a world where a bath once a week or even once a month was the norm.

The significance of the number of jars and their size is that the wine produced as a result of the miracle is a prodigious amount, far in excess of the demands of the wedding guests. Indeed that village community would enjoy the wine for months, perhaps even years to come. Moreover it would be exempt from tax and tithes.

On Jesus' instructions the huge stone jars (probably sunk into the ground to keep the water cool), are filled to capacity. A sample of the water, now wine, is then taken to the master of the banquet (v 8). In his enthusiasm he rushes off to find the bridegroom and to congratulate him on this splendid wine (v 10). So the water of Jewish tradition (v 6) becomes the vibrant wine of the Spirit.

No doubt the Johannine community saw in this miracle the end of Pharisaic or Essene Judaism and the beginning of the kind of Christianity which was experienced in their community. Their joy, exuberance and mutual love were the hallmarks of an experience in which they stepped out of dry formalism into the vitality of a living faith in Jesus. Their experience was, in a sense, a water-to-wine one, leaving behind the water of ritual washing for the wine of the eucharistic celebration. For them the experience was 'the best' (v 10).

The meaning of the miracle is now summed up (v 11). It is the first of Jesus' signs and it reveals his glory. The great worker of signs was Moses, and there are some scholars who believe that the 'signs' in the Gospel were once part of another work called the Signs Source, which they believe was written to show that Jesus was a kind of 'Second Moses'. Whether John has indeed taken over a Signs Source is debatable. If he has, it is now made into an integral part of his Gospel: these same signs are used to show Jesus' glory. What does this mean? The word *glory* has a rich Old Testament heritage and means sense of presence. When applied to God, the glory was visualized as smoke filling the temple or as a very bright light. In John, 'glory' refers to the revelation of Jesus' person, the glory of the one and only God (cf Jn 1:14 marginal note). In other words, the divinity of Jesus.

The disciples put their faith in Jesus (v 11b). This does not mean that they understand who he is or where he came from, but instinctively they trust him. In the days to come, as they get to know Jesus more fully, their commitment will grow. Those who weather the storms will at last, like Thomas, discover who Jesus really is. In looking back they will appreciate the signs. For the moment, however, their eyes are unable to penetrate the mystery of Jesus' glory.

Discussion

Several of our recent discussions had been rather intense, so we decided to keep this study light and informal. We therefore used the time to get to know each other, by telling the group about our own spiritual pilgrimage. We focused upon the question 'What difference does Jesus make in your life?' You may have other ideas for your own discussion. We found the answers to be frank and so we were drawn deeper into our relationship with each other. We finished by reading the reflection and using it to lead into a time of worship.

Reflection

When scholars turn from ancient texts
and the past fades out
so that present and future blend;
when life rushes in
through stained glass windows;
and faces break open
to let the people out;
when words become gestures,
love becomes tangible
and sorrow shared;
then we encounter
not just an empty tomb
but a risen Saviour.
Not the death of humanity
but a glorious Lord.

6. The Well

John 4:7-26

The group began the session with a discussion on jokes. We thought of different jokes and then classified them according to types. The two main categories were jokes about human weaknesses or appetites, and jokes about human stereotypes.

This opened the way for one of the group to speak about the Samaritans and to explain something of the friction which existed between them and the Jews. The Samaritans were forcibly excluded from the Jewish community during the time of Ezra and Nehemiah. The split began, not with the exile of the northern kingdom in 720 BC, but when the Samaritans were officially excluded from the new Judaism which Ezra brought from Babylon in c.428 BC. Alienated from friends and even family, the Samaritans went off into their own lonely exile. Wives and mothers were driven away from Judaism for no crime other than that they were Samaritans (cf Ezra 9 and 10 and Neh 13). So ethnicity replaced true religious conviction. We began to understand some of the pain felt by the Samaritans.

[7] When a Samaritan woman came to draw water, Jesus said to her, 'Will you give me a drink?'

[8] (His disciples had gone into the town to buy food.)

[9] The Samaritan woman said to him, 'You are a Jew and I am a Samaritan woman. How can you ask me for a drink?' (For Jews do not associate with Samaritans.)

[10] Jesus answered her, 'If you knew the gift of God and who it is that asks you for a drink, you would have asked him and he would have given you living water.'

[11] 'Sir,' the woman said, 'you have nothing to draw with and the well is deep. Where can you get this living water?

[12] Are you greater than our father Jacob, who gave us the well and drank from it himself, as did also his sons and his flocks and herds?'

[13] Jesus answered, 'Everyone who drinks this water will be thirsty again,

[14] but whoever drinks the water I give him will never thirst. Indeed, the water I give him will become in him a spring of water welling up to everlasting life.'

[15] The woman said to him, 'Sir, give me this water so that I won't get thirsty and have to keep coming here to draw water.'

[16] He told her, 'Go, call your husband and come back.'

[17] 'I have no husband,' she replied.

Jesus said to her, 'You are right when you say you have no husband.

[18] The fact is, you have had five husbands, and the man you now have is not your husband. What you have just said is quite true.'

[19] 'Sir,' the woman said, 'I can see that you are a prophet.

[20] Our fathers worshipped on this mountain, but you Jews claim that the place where we must worship is in Jerusalem.'

[21] Jesus declared, 'Believe me, woman, a time is coming when you will worship the Father neither on this mountain nor in Jerusalem.

[22] You Samaritans worship what you do not know; we worship what we do know, for salvation is from the Jews.

[23] Yet a time is coming and has now come when the true worshippers will worship the Father in spirit and truth, for they are the kind of worshippers the Father seeks.

²⁴ God is spirit, and his worshippers must worship in spirit and in truth.'

²⁵ The woman said, 'I know that Messiah' (called Christ) 'is coming. When he comes, he will explain everything to us.'

²⁶ Then Jesus declared, 'I who speak to you am he.'

Notes on the text

Background

The account of the miracle of the water turned to wine rests upon the conviction held by the Johannine community that their experience of God represented a new thing which God was doing in their age. This conviction leads John to the picture of Jesus as the Giver of Life. He uses different characters and events to draw out this theme. We shall look at three of these, beginning with the Samaritan woman.

News of Jesus' ministry in Judaea comes at last to the ears of the Pharisees (v 1). So begins the confrontation between Jesus and this group. (Remember that the reason John singles out the Pharisees as the enemies of Jesus is that they are also the chief opponents of the Johannine community.) In time Jesus will march right into the lion's den, but for the moment he needs to raise up a reliable group of disciples. So he takes refuge in the lonely hills of Galilee. He even avoids the usual route by taking the road through 'unclean' Samaria.

The total distance between Jerusalem and the Sea of Galilee is about a hundred and sixty kilometres or a hundred miles. It would take the disciples between three and five days depending on their speed. At midday, close to the halfway mark of the journey, they pause to buy food (v 5) at a village called Sychar (Asker) on the east slope of Mt Ebal. The mountain was identified by the Samaritans with Mt Moriah (cf Gen 22), and was believed to be the site of an altar erected by Joshua. Recent excavations on the mountain slope have revealed a curious structure which the discoverer insists is the same altar. Whether it is, is difficult to say. We do know that Mt Ebal like Mt Gerezim across the valley (containing the ruins of their temple, destroyed by the Jews) were sacred to the Samaritans. Leaving the holiest place of the Jews, Jesus now comes to the holiest place of the Samaritans.

Text

It is midday and summer, for Jesus had been in Jerusalem for Passover, which takes place in late spring. The scene is set and as the Samaritan woman approaches, a new act in our drama commences.

The well is about a kilometre from the village. This was sufficiently far away for it to be dangerous for a woman to walk there on her own. Was she avoiding the other women of the village by coming at mid-day on her own? Or was it just one of those days, when she had been too busy with the housework to get around to fetching water until it was needed for lunch? We don't know!

Jesus asks for water (v 7), and his accent betrays his Judaean origins. The woman is suprised (v 9) and a fascinating dialogue commences. The fact that Jesus' disciples have gone to buy food in a Samaritan village alerts us to something unusual. Most Jews would not eat that food (cf v 9b). Jesus and his disciples deliberately flout the ethnic barriers of the time. (Presumably John's community did the same and invited Samaritans and Gentiles into their midst.) Now Jesus addresses himself to a Samaritan woman, and one of questionable morality. He breaks not only the barriers of race, but also the barrier of sexual inequality and moral inferiority. This is John's equivalent to Jesus eating and drinking with tax collectors and prostitutes (cf Luke 5:30).

In v 10 Jesus introduces the idea of living water. In contrast to the still waters of the well, Jesus draws an image from the bubbling, cascading mountain streams of upper Galilee. Pure, fresh, sparkling, moving (living) water.

The woman mocks Jesus (v 11) in her gentle fashion. The well is deep, and he has no bucket. He could not reach the well water, never mind some mountain stream. There is a hint of sarcasm as she enquires whether Jesus thinks that he is greater than Jacob. According to Samaritan tradition Jacob was the founder of this well (v 12). The reader by this stage knows the answer. Jesus is greater than Jacob, just as he will show himself greater than the father of all Jews, namely Abraham (Jn 8:58).

Jesus shows his greatness by contrasting the waters of the well with the eternal life which he brings the believers (vv 13,14). Out of their very being (lit. their belly), spring water will gush forth, bringing them eternal life. The imagery sounds strange, but the gist is clear. The outside (well) water is not as useful as a spring of water on the inside. Especially since the inside water brings with it eternal life.

The complexity of the imagery causes the woman to misunderstand (v 15) and this in turn allows Jesus to restate his message in more detail. This is a common feature in John's Gospel, where through the misunderstanding of one of the characters the reader is enabled to think through an issue from a number of different perspectives. Both Nicodemus and the Samaritan woman understand the words of Jesus on the literal plane, so enhancing, for the reader, the spiritual meaning.

Verses 16-18 swing the focus directly upon the woman and her personal life. At the moment she has no husband, only a lover, but there is no overtone of judgement in Jesus' voice. Gently Jesus pinpoints the woman's tragic and hitherto abortive quest for meaning and fulfilment. Jesus' words, full of insight, will later form the basis for her witness to her village (v 29).

The woman then confesses that Jesus is a prophet (v 19), and uses this information to bring in a theological issue (v 20). The same issue had split the Jewish/ Samaritan population of Alexandria in the previous century, and was still alive in New Testament times. Which was the holy mountain of God, Jerusalem chosen by David or the twin Mt Ebal and Mt Gerezim chosen by Moses (Jos 8)? Which mountain was the sacred Mt Moriah, where Abraham offered Isaac? The Jews claimed Jerusalem, the Samaritans claimed Gerezim. The roots of the whole disagreement lay in the sixth century, when the Samaritans were no longer allowed to participate in the Jewish temple, and even their offer of help to rebuild the temple was rejected (Ezra 4:1-4). The Samaritans were then forced to build their own temple on Mt Gerezim (opposite Mt Ebal). This temple was destroyed by the Jews in 128 BC, when John Hyrcanus captured Shechem. The memory was obviously still a painful one for the Samaritans.

The debate was obviously known to John and his readers, and may even have been an issue in their community, since there seem to have been both Jews and Samaritans present. It also provides the ideal opportunity for John to teach the reader an important lesson, as he shows Jesus cutting through the debate with a blunt statement of truth. The proud temple of Jerusalem will fall as did the temple of Mt Gerezim (v 21). The readers of course know that this prophecy has come true: the Jewish temple is already in ruins by the time John writes the Gospel.

Jesus confirms the truth of Judaism (v 22). The Samaritans are limited in the knowledge of God, because they only have one third of the Scriptures (ie Genesis to Deuteronomy). Indeed they know almost nothing of the expected Messiah, hence Jesus' words, 'Salvation is from the Jews'. It is from the Jewish Bible that the full picture of the promised salvation may be obtained. Remember that the Bible of the early Christians was the Old Testament until well into the second century AD.

Jesus also limits the Jewish claim by the 'yet' of v 23. Judaism has been superseded by Jesus and his unique role as the revealer of God (Jn 1:17). The Johannine community lives in a new age, the age of the Spirit. 'The time is coming' is the perspective of the Jesus of history; 'and now is' is the perspective of John's readers. Even now, they experience a new form of worship, which is more free than the traditional worship of the temples, with its sacrifices and washings. Beyond the ruins of the Jerusalem temple and the shattered hopes of Jewish nationalism, lies a new era — the age of the Church.

Today, the Samaritans still carry out their worship, their sacrifices and the ancient traditions, on the same sites as of old. Reduced to less than a hundred and fifty persons, they still maintain their ethnic purity, and bear the scars of their rejection of over two thousand years ago. They worship what they do not know (v 22). What a contrast lies here with the spirit directed worship of which Jesus speaks (vv 23-5).

'In spirit and truth' (v 23). The whole Gospel rests upon the right understanding of these two words. Truth indicates right teaching, which comes from a right understanding of who Jesus is. Spirit is the experience of the guiding presence of the Spirit within the community. Truth and Spirit meet at the point of the community's worship of the divine and ever-present Jesus. To worship God 'in spirit and truth' is to respond in worship to the divine Jesus, and to recognize the role of the Spirit in leading people into all truth (Jn 16:13) by reminding Christians of the words of Jesus (Jn 16:14).

The woman has recognized Jesus as a prophet, now she encounters another dimension to him. He is the Messiah (v 26). Samaritans expected a prophet like Moses (cf Deut 18:18), who would bring in a new revelation of God. The woman uses the basic Samaritan idea of a revealer (v 25), but prefers the Jewish title 'Messiah'. In other words, the woman has now transcended her Samaritan background. We may be sure that by the time John writes, many Samaritans have walked this way (cf Acts 8:25), and have come to recognize Jesus as Messiah. But there is more, as always in John.

The witness of the woman leads the villagers to make a united confession of faith in Jesus (v 42). He is the Saviour, not just of the Jews, but of the world. The ethnic confines of the Jewish nationalistic messiah are shattered. The universal message of Jesus escapes and the walls between nation and nation, race and race, colour and colour collapse. Those three words 'of the world' sound the death knell for every regime which dares to divide people by race, colour or class.

Discussion

We began our discussion by asking what the significance was, that led John to use a Samaritan, a woman of doubtful reputation, as the main character in this key story. We then asked ourselves whether there were any guidelines here for Christian work in communities of outcasts. One of the group referred to the work of Gandhi among the harijans (outcasts) of India. Gandhi had seen this as a major issue, even before the independence of India. So he campaigned for the opening of Hindu temples to these people and frequently lived among them. The hardest lesson his wife had to learn was when it was her turn to clean the harijan latrines. Are there outcasts in our community? What are we doing about them? Do we consider them when we work for a better future for our country?

Reflection

Her gaunt face peered through wispy hair prematurely grey. She smoothed her too tight dress, chasing wrinkles with her hand. Tired eyes watched the passing parade, searching out the customers from the curious. Inwardly she cursed the system which held her captive. The men who had enslaved her to their passions left her dead and cold inside. They no longer even looked in her eyes, only her body mattered and that was now growing old. Yet she was only twenty-two years old. How she longed for someone who was different, a person who would love her for what she was inside — the poet, the singer, the mother, the lover, the friend. But people like that never looked her way. They passed her by as if she were invisible, the same way they ignored the outstretched hands of the drunk and the street urchin. What a pity Christians were not more like Jesus, she thought.

7. The Hillside

John 6:8-15, 32-34

We began the evening by sharing together a meal which was modelled upon the Jewish traditional Sabbath meal with a few variations. We all stood to say grace at the beginning. (Traditionally, only the men stand, but we chose to be different.) After reading the Biblical text one of our group took some of the bread rolls, broke them into sizeable portions and handed them out. Later in the meal we said grace again, this time specifically for the gift of grapes, the fruit of the vine. A common cup was circulated. At the end of the meal we sang a few Christian songs, focusing upon the kingship of Jesus.

[8] **Another of his disciples, Andrew, Simon Peter's brother, spoke up,**

[9] **'Here is a boy with five small barley loaves and two small fish, but how far will they go among so many?'**

[10] **Jesus said, 'Have the people sit down.' There was plenty of grass in that place, and the men sat down, about five thousand of them.**

[11] **Jesus then took the loaves, gave thanks, and distributed to those who were seated as much as they wanted. He did the same with the fish.**

[12] **When they had all had enough to eat, he said to his disciples, 'Gather the pieces that are left over. Let nothing be wasted.'**

[13] **So they gathered them and filled twelve baskets with the pieces of the five barley loaves left over by those who had eaten.**

[14] **After the people saw the miraculous sign that Jesus did, they began to say: 'Surely this is the Prophet who is to come into the world.'**

[15] **Jesus, knowing that they intended to come and make him king by force, withdrew again into the hills by himself.**

[32] **Jesus said to them, 'I tell you the truth, it is not Moses who has given you the bread from heaven, but it is my Father who gives you the true bread from heaven.**

[33] **For the bread of God is he who comes down from heaven and gives life to the world.'**

[34] **'Sir,' they said, 'from now on gives us this bread.'**

Notes on the text

Background

John writes his Gospel as if it were a drama. Thus he introduces each scene with a short description of the time and place, as a narrator might do in a play. In John 6, we encounter just such a description in the opening verses. We read that it is springtime and Jesus is out in the Galilean countryside. For his own safety and that of the disciples, Jesus prefers to avoid the towns and cities of the area. Later he will in fact take refuge in the desert (Jn 10:40 and 11:54). A person of the calibre of Jesus would soon attract the attention of the Roman representative (the prefect Pontius Pilate), so Jesus knew his time was very limited.

Josephus, the Jewish historian, describes the savage attacks of the Romans on the unarmed and largely defenceless crowds who turned out to follow one of the 'messianic' figures who appeared from time to time: the people accompanied one such 'messiah' into the Judaean desert, where he had promised to bring manna from heaven, like Moses of old. No manna came, but the Romans descended instead and slaughtered many thousands of innocent men, women and children. Their crime? Looking for God's messenger, who like Moses would perform signs and wonders for the people. But in Roman eyes, the combination of a charismatic figure and a crowd spelt revolution — some things never change!

Jesus needs time to build up a responsible group of followers, and this means keeping a low profile. Galilee, being under Herod and not under direct Roman rule, was much safer than Judaea. But even in Galilee the Roman presence was felt, especially in the cities like Tiberius and Sepphoris. We discover that Jesus' fame is spreading and a crowd of people gather around him (v 2) having heard about his previous miracles. Can he be the Messiah who performs signs and wonders like Moses did?

Try to imagine the sense of nervousness and expectancy — rather like sitting in church listening to Alan Boesak (or Martin Luther King), while the police patrol the streets outside. The disciples were probably all too eager to come to an end and send the people home (cf Luke 9:12). Here in John, it is Jesus who introduces the notion of feeding the people (v 6), in a teasing comment to Philip. Philip quickly points out that it is beyond their slender resources (v 7).

Text
Andrew, who brought Peter to Jesus, now brings forward a boy and his lunch (v 8). Obviously he has the gift of finding useful people. The

boy's lunch (v 9) is a typical peasant meal of cheap barley rolls and a couple of fish. Given the smallness of the meal, one wonders why Andrew even bothered to bring the boy to Jesus. Perhaps the boy was very persistent, or Andrew thought that Jesus might give the boy a special blessing for his kind thought.

Jesus takes Andrew's ironic remark quite seriously. He instructs the people, through the disciples, to be seated (v 10). The hill slopes with their covering of green grass create a comfortable picnic spot. Mark describes the ordering of the people by hundreds and fifties (Mk 6:40), which has a decidedly military ring about it. John leaves that detail out, but the revolutionary aspect hovers in the background, to emerge in v 15.

Jesus takes the loaves, gives thanks (*eucharisteisas*) and distributes the food to the people (v 11). The disciples' part is not mentioned (unlike Mark 6:41), which leaves the reader with the impression that Jesus gives the food directly to each person present. This has the effect of reminding the reader of the Last Supper and the institution of the eucharist. John is quite secretive about the sacred mysteries of the Christian church, like baptism and the eucharist. He prefers to allude to rather than to speak openly about them, and so protects these rites from being desecrated either by word or deed. To the knowing reader, the story of the feeding of the crowd and the teaching of Jesus which comes later in the chapter (vv 51-59) are sufficient reminder that the celebration of the eucharist is rooted in the fellowship which Jesus enjoyed with his followers.

The directness of Jesus' feeding also tells us something about John's understanding of ministry. No priesthood interposes between Jesus and the believer. No hierarchy of Christian leaders mediates between Jesus and the worshippers. This directness could only grow out of an experience of the Holy Spirit in which each and every believer found for themselves the presence of Jesus. This personal sense of fellowship and contact must have militated against any attempt to impose a pattern of inequality on the believers. What a different church would the Christian church have been had it followed the Johannine model instead of the hierarchy of clergy and laity.

The food is sufficient for all and at this stage the disciples are given a role in the story, to collect the broken pieces of bread (v 12). This gathering role illustrates the difference between the Christian task of bringing people to Jesus, and Jesus' task as the giver of life. As the disciples gather the fragments into the baskets, so the beloved disciple gathered the Johannine community about him.

The miracle is a 'sign' of Jesus, the third to be so described since the wedding. Now the people remember the promise (Deut 18:18) of a prophet like Moses. Surely this miracle of Jesus must be confirmation that he is that prophet (v 14), for he has fed the people in this lonely place. This is surely just what the rabbis meant when they said that the Messiah would perform the miracles of Moses and supply both bread and water for the community of the new age.

In the mind of the crowd, the transition from prophet to king (v 15) quickly takes place, and the realization that Jesus is a likely candidate for a revolutionary leader grips the people. Eyes are filled with visions of victorious battles over the hated Romans. Ears can already hear the cries of triumph and the screams of the dying Romans. Hands reach out to catch Jesus and make him into the king of their dreams. But suddenly, their eyes are opened, their ears unstopped as their hands clutch at empty air. Jesus has gone!

In the discourse which follows and takes up most of chapter 6, Jesus demonstrates his superiority over Moses (v 32), for he is himself the living bread which comes down from heaven (v 33). To a world facing the terrible prospect of death, Jesus comes to bring eternal life. To people without meaning in life (the living dead), Jesus brings a new sense of being, belonging and purpose. To people, like the Jews, struggling with the Law of Moses, Jesus brings a message of forgiveness and hope — a new revelation as fresh and exciting as the wine of Cana.

Discussion

We focused our discussion on the Incarnation, and the way in which Jesus took on human form and lived among ordinary people, sharing their joys and their sorrows. We then went on to think about ways in which the Church could perform a similar service.

These are some of the suggestions which we made:
1 Supporting the families of striking workers, both financially and in prayer.
2 White Christians living in black communities, even if only for short periods of time, and so learning to see life through their eyes. One

young Christian spoke about the warmth and love he had encountered during his stay in Soweto.

3 Attending funerals of people killed in police or army action.

4 Attending trials to ensure that any discrimination is reported.

5 Praying for people jailed because of their Christian commitment.

Your group will need to reflect on this in response to your own context and circumstances.

Reflection

As the northern parts of India erupted into a violent civil war between Muslims and Hindus, the hope of rational dialogue died. Children, even babies, were brutally killed. Some were torn limb from limb. A well, choked with the bodies of young women who had committed suicide in preference to rape, told its own appalling story. Hate on hate, murder on murder, rape on rape and as the men fought on, the women and children bled to death in the streets.

Then Mahatma Gandhi came, with his disciples. They went out, singly, to live as Hindus in Muslim villages, preaching, teaching, but mostly praying. After three or four days in one village, they would move on to another. All the time they faced death, injury, and repeated waves of anger, but that did not stop them nor diminish the love which they carried in their hearts. When one disciple fell ill with malaria, he requested that his sister, a doctor in a nearby village, be sent to nurse him. Gandhi responded that 'those who go to the villages have to go with a determination to live or die there'. The doctor was duty bound to her own village and would not be allowed to break that commitment. That was the standard which Gandhi had set himself. Jesus demands a similar commitment from his present day disciples!

JESUS, THE JUDGE

The judgement of Jesus is a frightening concept, for it reminds us of the fearful judgement of God that blazes out time and again within the Old Testament record. From the thunder of Mt Sinai and the death of the Egyptian first-born to the punishment of the people in the terrible exile to Assyria and Babylonia, the picture is the same. 'It is a dreadful thing to fall into the hands of the living God' says the author of Hebrews (10:31).

In John, judgement follows a meeting with Jesus, and a particular revelation about him. The Greek word for judgement is *'krisis'*, from which we derive the English word crisis. Indeed the very presence of Jesus creates a crisis which demands a response. This may be either a confession of belief in him, or rejection and disbelief. The promise of eternal life is given to those who confess belief, while the threat of judgement rests upon those who reject Jesus. We have considered several of the confessions; now we turn to those people who either do not make an adequate confession of faith or who reject Jesus completely. These studies will allow us to come to understand something of the picture of Jesus as judge.

The theme of judgement is introduced in ch 3 of the Gospel, and given extensive treatment in ch 5. We discover a number of important details there:

1 To meet with Jesus is to experience already in this life something of the final judgement. Belief in Jesus results in a movement from judgement into eternal life (5:24). So depending on one's response to Jesus, one is either marked for reward or for punishment, life or death.

2 The authority of judgement is given to Jesus because he is the Son of Man (Child of Humanity), as we see in 5:27. The reference is to the figure described in Daniel 7:13, and to the thrones for judgement mentioned in vv 9f. Clearly Daniel envisaged an eschatological judge who looked like a human being. Perhaps he had in mind the angel Michael. In later Jewish literature produced about the same time as John's Gospel (eg 1 Enoch), the Son of Man is seen to be one of the judges whom God appoints for the final judgement.

3 The accuser in the judgement which Jesus brings upon the Pharisees is not Satan or Jesus but Moses (5:45). In other words, the record of written revelation attests to the truth of Jesus. To ignore this testimony, is to face judgement by that very same testimony.

The writer has in mind the people who threaten his community, namely the Pharisees of his time. They read the scriptures knowing that therein lies the path to eternal life, but they fail to see that the scriptures point to Jesus (5:39). Claiming to be the disciples of Moses (9:28), they are in fact the children of the devil (8:44). Harsh words, but rising out of a terrible conflict in which the Johannine community was fighting for its very existence (1 Jn 5:19)!

The theme of judgement returns in ch 9 and there, as so often in John, it is accompanied by a reference to light and darkness (9:4f, 39-41). The light of Jesus' judgement blazes in the dark, exposing evil (3:20). A blind man receives his sight, and the Pharisees turn out to be spiritually blind.

The idea of disbelief returns in ch 12, where we discover that not only did Isaiah see Jesus' divine glory (12:41), but he also foretold the rejection of Jesus on the part of the Jewish leaders (12:37-40). Obviously John was deeply pained by that rejection as, daily, he and the other members of the community struggled to bring the Christian faith to their Jewish friends and family. Some paid the price, but many preferred to remain as secret believers. The cost of following Jesus was too high (12:42).

Just as the words of the Old Testament and in particular the Law of Moses act as the judge of the Pharisees, so the words of Jesus are themselves the judge of all those who hear them but do not put them into practice (12:48). The judgement of Jesus descends upon both the world and the Church.

Finally lest the reader gain the impression that the mission of Jesus is solely or even primarily to bring judgement, Jesus says 'I did not come to judge the world but to save it' (Jn 12:47). The essence of Jesus' mission is one of salvation, one of light and life. But there will always be those who prefer darkness and on them the judgement of scripture and the living words of Jesus will fall.

8. The Verdict

John 3:1-21

We began the session by talking about the things which distinguish Christians from non-Christians. In other words, the marks of a Christian. The group quickly pointed out the obvious things, like attending a church or concern for matters like prayer or Bible study. Then we came to those areas which were less obvious, like personal attitudes and convictions. This raised the question about how open one should be about one's Christian convictions. Thus we came to consider the question of secret disciples. We read John 12:37-43 and tried to imagine what it would have been like to have been one of these 'secret disciples'. Why were they so afraid of excommunication from the synagogue? Did they really prefer the praise of people to the praise of God (Jn 12:43)?

³ In reply Jesus declared, 'I tell you the truth, unless a man is born again, he cannot see the kingdom of God.'

⁴ 'But,' said Nicodemus, 'how can a man be born when he is old? Surely he cannot enter a second time into his mother's womb to be born!'

⁵ Jesus answered, 'I tell you the truth, unless a man is born of water and the Spirit, he cannot enter the kingdom of God.

⁶ Flesh gives birth to flesh, but the Spirit gives birth to spirit.

⁷ You should not be surprised at my saying, "You must be born again."

⁸ The wind blows wherever it pleases. You may hear its sound, but you cannot tell where it comes from or where it is going. So it is with everyone born of the Spirit.'

⁹ 'How can this be?' Nicodemus asked.

¹⁰ 'You are a teacher of Israel,' said Jesus, 'and do you not understand these things?

¹¹ I tell you the truth, we speak of what we know, and we testify to what we have seen, but still you people do not accept our testimony.

¹² I have spoken to you of earthly things and you do not believe; how then will you believe if I speak of heavenly things?

¹³ No one has ever gone into heaven except the one who came from heaven — the Son of Man.

¹⁴ Just as Moses lifted up the snake in the desert, so the Son of Man must be lifted up,

¹⁵ that everyone who believes may have eternal life in him.

¹⁶ 'For God so loved the world that he gave his one and only Son, that whoever believes in him shall not perish but have everlasting life.

¹⁷ For God did not send his Son into the world to condemn the world, but to save the world through him.

¹⁸ Whoever believes in him is not condemned, but whoever does not believe stands condemned already because he has not believed in the name of God's one and only Son.

¹⁹ This is the verdict: Light has come into the world, but men loved darkness instead of light because their deeds were evil.
²⁰ Everyone who does evil hates the light, and will not come into the light for fear that his deeds will be exposed.
²¹ But whoever lives by the truth comes into the light, so that it may be seen plainly that what he has done has been done through God.'

Notes on the text

Background

The chapter opens with the usual introductory notes. We meet a new character in the story of Jesus, whose Greek name is Nicodemus. We are not told his Hebrew name, which may suggest that John is protecting this man, or his memory, from possible Jewish action. His description as a Pharisee and member of the Sanhedrin (the Jewish high court and parliament), suggests that he is a person of considerable importance. We remember that the Pharisees were the chief opponents of the Johannine community, and in this Gospel the leaders of the opposition against Jesus. One of the secondary themes of the Gospel is the consistent attempt on the part of the Pharisees ('the Jews') to find Jesus guilty and to execute him for blasphemy (cf Jn 10:33).

Nicodemus comes to Jesus by night (v 2). The last phrase puts him into the category of the 'secret disciples' (Jn 12:42), one of the followers of Jesus who refuse to confess Jesus openly as the Messiah for fear of excommunication. We know that John is very critical of these people (cf Jn 12:43). Nicodemus in fact does not fare well in the Gospel, as this initial meeting with Jesus will show.

He greets Jesus as a fellow rabbi (v 2) and as a teacher, inspired by God. The faith of Nicodemus rests upon the signs which Jesus has done (v 2b). Here lies a problem, for that kind of faith often results in a misunderstanding of the true nature of Jesus (eg Jn 6:14f and cf 2:23-5). Nicodemus turns out to be no exception to this rule. He apparently views Jesus as a kind of miracle worker, a prophet, but nothing more. Later in John 7:50-52 where Nicodemus reappears, the issue remains the prophetic nature of Jesus.

Jesus responds to the words of Nicodemus, by making an ambiguous statement (v 3). One may understand the Greek word *anothen* as 'above' or as 'again'. Jesus is saying that unless one is born from above, that is spiritually, one cannot enter (see) the kingdom of God. Jesus comes from above and, by means of the Spirit, opens up a way for all people to be born into the family of God (1 Jn 5:1).

Nicodemus understands *anothen* as again, and thinks that Jesus is saying he must be literally born again. Hence his ridiculous question in v 4. The reader can but smile in pity at this great teacher grappling with the simple teaching of Jesus. We begin to have an inkling of what it means to be spiritually blind.

Jesus clarifies the issue (vv 5 and 6), by referring to the idea of spiritual birth over against natural (water) birth. The slightly unusual reference to natural birth as water birth, reminds the reader of the Jewish understanding of baptism as a kind of birth into Judaism. (Non Jews were baptized as a sign that they were leaving their old life and family behind them and entering into a new life as Jews. This is called proselyte baptism and is still practised today.) There is a contrast here (as in ch 1:31-34) between the water baptism of Jewish tradition (also practised by the Christians) and the Spirit baptism which Jesus alone brings (Jn 1:33).

Jesus introduces a further complicating factor into the discussion when he speaks about wind and spirit in the same breath (vv 7 and 8). In both Greek and Hebrew, one word is used for both concepts. So if you were translating this passage from Greek you would have to rely on the sense to know which of these ideas Jesus intends at a particular point in the two verses.

Nicodemus is confused (v 9) and Jesus gently rebukes him (v 10). At this point the discussion becomes a monologue, Nicodemus is forgotten. The introduction of 'we' into the conversation at v 11 suggests that this is the combined voice of Jesus and the Johannine community. We have told you (the Jews) about what we know from our own experience, and what we have seen, but still 'you' (the Jews) do not accept 'our' testimony.

Verse 12 introduces a contrast between earthly and heavenly things. If Nicodemus and those whom he represents fail to understand the earthly words of Jesus, how will they understand the heavenly things which he says. In other words, if they are deaf to the words spoken by Jesus while he was on earth, how will they listen to the words of Jesus which the Spirit brings to later generations (Jn 14:26). Jesus then affirms his authority to act as the agent of spiritual things. He has come from heaven (v 13) for he is the Child of Humanity (Son of Man), the mysterious stranger on earth. Some very old manuscripts add the words 'who is in heaven'. This is in line with the perspective of the Johannine community, for Jesus is now in heaven.

The monologue turns to the death of Jesus. He must be lifted up so that those who believe may have eternal life *in him* (v 14f). Outside of Jesus there is no life, only judgement. There is a pun on the words 'lifted up', which reminds one of the cross, but also of John's presentation of Jesus' death as his exaltation (Jn 13:31f). Jesus is God's gift of life to a dying world (v 16). God in love sends Jesus not as a judge, although the world deserves that, but as a saviour (v 17). Nevertheless a sense of judgement is still present. Belief in Jesus is the only correct response to the initiative of God. Those who like Martha, Mary and Peter believe in Jesus will pass from judgement into life (5:24). Those who do not confess belief in Jesus will be condemned (v 18).

Then comes the verdict of God on the world. Jesus has brought light into the world, but people have rejected that light in preference for their evil ways (v 19). Indeed those people hate the light and will not come to Jesus for fear that their evil ways will be exposed (v 20). Only those, like the Johannine community, who live by the truth (that is they live in accordance with the dictates of God's Spirit), come to Jesus. The light of God is reflected in their lives for the world to see (v 20), but the world, like Nicodemus, is blind and confused.

Discussion

We spent some time speaking about Nicodemus, wondering what kind of person he was. We read John 19:39, where Nicodemus donates more than enough spices for Jesus' burial. Did he find faith at last? Or was he left with the remembrance of the dead Jesus? The writer leaves us to puzzle out our own solution.

We then went on to speak about the reluctance of so many Christians to take sides in contemporary political issues. Many would rather obey the state and its laws than stand up against injustice and evil. We realized that we were all part of that group in some ways. Fear of the authorities make us secret disciples, and forces us into silence. We too are guilty of preferring popularity to the praise of God (cf Jn 12:43). After a time of prayer together, we read the reflection and discussed its meaning for us today. Perhaps you might choose for reflection a passage which relates to your own society.

Reflection

As the prison gates slammed closed behind the little convoy, Mkelo wondered where they were taking him. Two months in prison had aged the thirteen year old. At first there had been only the cold, dark, lonely nights filled with body-wracking sobs. Now he had grown out of tears, and the cold fear which had lain like a shroud upon him had been replaced by a smouldering anger.

The truck drove out of the city limits and eventually turned in at a set of wire gates. Razor wire surrounded the stockade and a sign proclaimed it a Youth Camp. Mkelo was in one of the re-education camps for young black political prisoners arrested during the state of emergency. To his surprise the camp was staffed by a group of non-military personnel who came from a nearby white church. 'What are these Christians doing here?' he wondered. But as he listened to their talk, to their attacks on black violence and their support of the actions of the police and army, Mkelo became even more confused. They used their Christianity to break down the young people's commitment to change. They presented a Jesus who was silent, passive and largely indifferent to the plight of the blacks. Indeed one to whom their souls were all that mattered!

Mkelo realized that these people had made Jesus into a rich, white, western intellectual. In his suffering he could not identify with that Jesus, nor with these Christians who served the ends of an evil regime.

9. Light that Blinds

John 9:1-7, 13-14, 24-29, and 35-39

The group began the session with a simple candlelight ceremony. A cardboard box filled with sand was placed in the centre of the room, on a small table. A container of candles was nearby. A single candle was lit and placed upright in the box and all the lights were put off. We then read the set passage on Jesus the Judge.

One by one, we picked up a candle, lit it from the first candle and placed it in the sandbox. At the same time, we each told the group about one significant event in our lives as Christians, which related to the theme of witness. For example, we spoke about times when we had to stand up for our faith, or when we had challenged someone about their actions. Others spoke about the way God had challenged them about a particular matter. So our candle became a sign of that event. Rather a solemn occasion. (You may choose to do the study first and end with this ceremony.)

¹ As he went along, he saw a man blind from birth.

² His disciples asked him, 'Rabbi, who sinned, this man or his parents, that he was born blind?'

³ 'Neither this man nor his parents sinned,' said Jesus, 'but this happened so that the work of God might be displayed in his life.

⁴ As long as it is day, we must do the work of him who sent me. Night is coming, when no one can work.

⁵ While I am in the world, I am the light of the world.'

⁶ Having said this, he spat on the ground, made some mud with the saliva, and put it on the man's eyes.

⁷ 'Go,' he told him, 'wash in the pool of Siloam' (this word means Sent). So the man went and washed, and came home seeing.

¹³ They brought to the Pharisees the man who had been blind.

¹⁴ Now the day on which Jesus made the mud and opened the man's eyes was a Sabbath.

²⁴ A second time they summoned the man who had been blind. 'Give glory to God,' they said. 'We know this man is a sinner.'

²⁵ He replied, 'Whether he is a sinner or not, I don't know. One thing I do know: I was blind but now I see!'

²⁶ Then they asked him, 'What did he do to you? How did he open your eyes?'

²⁷ He answered, 'I have told you already and you did not listen. Why do you want to hear it again? Do you want to become his disciples, too?'

²⁸ Then they hurled insults at him and said, 'You are this fellow's disciple! We are disciples of Moses!

²⁹ We know that God spoke to Moses, but as for this fellow, we don't even know where he comes from.'

³⁵ Jesus heard that they had thrown him out, and when he found him, he said, 'Do you believe in the Son of Man?'

³⁶ 'Who is he, sir?' the man asked. 'Tell me so that I may believe in him.'

³⁷ Jesus said, 'You have now seen him; in fact, he is the one speaking with you.'

³⁸ Then the man said, 'Lord, I believe,' and he worshipped him.

³⁹ Jesus said, 'For judgement I have come into this world, so that the blind will see and those who see will turn out to be blind.'

Notes on the text

Background

Jesus goes up to Jerusalem to celebrate the festival of Tabernacles along with thousands of other pilgrims (Jn 7:1-14). Three times a year, at Passover, Pentecost and Tabernacles, the holy city trebled in population as the throng of pilgrims from all over the world flocked in.

Tabernacles was originally a harvest festival and the making of booths (temporary shelters) reflects the ancient tradition of the workers living out in the fields until the harvesting was completed. Often the whole community would assist the farmers of the area and the end of the harvest would be celebrated with great joy and plenty of food and wine. Tabernacles was also the time of the new year celebration, when Jewish legend held that the fates of the coming year were decided by God and the angels. Each person could expect to be rewarded or punished on the basis of the life they had led in the year past. Fertility, safety, and wealth were the signs of blessing. Obviously this was a very good time for Jesus to speak to the people about judgement.

Three interesting ceremonies took place at Tabernacles. Firstly, the people processed around the altar waving small tree branches in their hands. Originally this ceremony may have been related to the celebration of the sovereignty of God. At least one of the Dead Sea Scrolls (scroll 11Q Melchizedek from Qumran) connects Tabernacles and the sovereignty of God. Secondly, the priests lit a gigantic menorah (lampstand), which from its place in the temple courts could be seen from all over Jerusalem. Thirdly, water was poured on the altar by the high priest and a prayer was said to God for the speedy arrival of the autumn rains.

The combination of light and judgement at this festival forms a very suitable basis for the teaching of Jesus on the dangers of rejecting his message. In John 8:12, Jesus describes himself as the light of the world. Those people who follow him will never walk in darkness, but will have the light of eternal life. Jesus, like the great lampstand of the temple, lights the way from darkness into the very presence of God.

In ch 9, John tells a story about a blind man. The intention of the story is more than just to recount an event in the life of Jesus. As we read the story we become conscious of the overlap between the history of Jesus and the history of the Johannine community. In fact ch 9 is their story, and describes their own history from their origins in the synagogue, through the pain of their excommunication and their amazing discovery of Jesus outside the confines of orthodox Judaism. In other words, the blind man represents the community's search for faith.

Text

John introduces the blind man (v 1), name unknown, and the disciples use the occasion for a theological debate (v 2). Is the man blind because he sinned somehow in his mother's womb? Or is his blindness a result of the sin of his parents? The orthodox Jewish understanding of misfortune as a direct consequence of one's sins or the sins of one's parents is presupposed here. Jesus sees the occasion not as a moment for an abstract theological discussion but as a time for practical help. He shortcircuits the discussion and prepares to heal the man (v 3). Night is coming, prophesies Jesus, when I will no longer be here in human form to help you (v 4). The Johannine community well knew that darkness, when they thought that Jesus had abandoned them, when the waves of persecution and opposition began to rise about them.

In the midst of such darkness, sorrow, suffering and oppression, Jesus is the light (v 5). Jesus' role as light is not confined to his human ministry. The early Christians knew the ongoing presence of the Holy Spirit (Jesus' alter ego — his other self). It was that discovery which had given the Johannine community the courage to face the darkness of despair and rise above the waves which threatened to engulf them. Jesus was still with them (Jn 14:19).

Jesus heals the blind man (vv 6-8) and we listen to the initial testimony of the man (v 11). The fact that the man knows only that Jesus is a person who works miracles, marks the very first stage of his move from ignorance into faith. Here he stands side by side with Nicodemus (cf 3:2), acknowledging Jesus as a kind of prophet. Unlike the Pharisee, the once blind man will not stay at that point, but will press on to discover the full truth about Jesus.

Pat Holo

The man's testimony continues. *First* he describes the healing (v 15) and confesses Jesus to be a prophet (v 17b). We begin to realize that the whole discussion is taking the shape of a trial. The blind man, and indirectly Jesus, are being tried by the Pharisees. The next witnesses in the case, after the accused, are his parents (v 18). They refuse to speak on behalf of their adult son (v 21), because they are afraid (v 22f). An ominous note creeps in. The threat of excommunication looms large against any Jew who confesses Jesus as the Messiah.

In about 85 AD, the Jewish rabbis of the central council of Jamnia (Galilee) introduced the so-called Twelfth Benediction into the daily liturgy of the synagogue. The gist of the 'blessing' was in fact a curse aimed against heretics. Although not specifically against Christians, it had the effect of making it impossible for Christians to worship in the synagogue. Unless, of course, they became secret disciples (Jn 12:42f) refusing to make an open confession of faith — just like the parents of the blind man. This chapter gives us some idea of the way in which the leaders of the synagogues put pressure on Christians to conform or face excommunication and the consequent loss of family and often financial ties.

The *second* appearance of the blind man before the Pharisees begins in v 24. This time the debate revolves around Jesus' apparently sinful nature (v 24). The Johannine Christians believed of course that Jesus' divine nature made him sinless, but this was a great point of controversy between the Christians and the Jews. The discussion paves the way for the blind man to make a wonderful confession of faith. 'One thing I do know; I was blind but now I see!' (v 25). Indeed before the chapter is finished we shall discover that this seeing has a spiritual dimension to it.

To the repeated question on the 'how' of the miracle, the man enquires whether the Pharisees want to become Jesus' disciples also (v 27). The 'also' is significant for it implies that the blind man intends to follow Jesus. Indeed, in the opinion of the Pharisees, he is already a disciple (v 28). They insult him (v 28) and a contrast emerges between the disciples of Moses and the disciples of Jesus. A perfect description of the difference between the Synagogue community and the Johannine community. We sense that the struggle between the two concerns questions of authority and power, and the major issue of the person of Jesus.

Verse 29 sums up the Synagogue's view of Jesus. God spoke to Moses, but this Jesus — why they do not even know where he comes from! The mockery in the voices of the Pharisees as they dismiss the humble origins of Jesus' earthly home, reveals their lack of knowledge about his heavenly origins. Jesus, the stranger from heaven, is the object of their mirth for they cannot see beyond his human form. They are blinded by their own 'knowledge'. Yet if they had read the words of Moses, they would have found that these words testify to Jesus (Jn 5:46).

The man now proceeds to fault the logic of the Pharisees (vv 30-33). Perhaps he uses the very arguments which the Johannine community would later use to try to convince their Jewish counterparts. The result is a final confrontation and the man's excommunication (v 34). The reference to 'steeped in sin at birth' looks back to the debate about sin in the opening verses of the chapter. The Pharisees understand blindness as the consequence of some sort of sin. In fact it is spiritual blindness not physical blindness which is related to sin.

Jesus finds the man (v 35), just as he found the Johannine community after their own expulsion from the Synagogue. 'Do you believe in the Son of Man?' asks Jesus. The man responds in faith but without understanding. So Jesus reveals in v 37 that he is the Son of Man (Child of Humanity), which in this Gospel is tantamount to a revelation of the divinity of Jesus. Not only does the man acknowledge Jesus as Lord, he worships him (v 38). Thus he affirms Jesus' divinity and so prepares the reader for the confessions of Thomas and Martha.

The blind man has moved from his understanding of Jesus as a prophet and worker of miracles (17b), to his confession of Jesus as Messiah (implicit in v 34), and to the final acknowledgement of Jesus as divine (v 38). This was the same path which the Johannine community took, as they followed the leading of the Holy Spirit to prepare the whole of Christendom for the doctrine of the Trinity. To understand this movement from primitive Christology to the full acknowledgement of Jesus' divine oneness with God, is to understand the heart of John's Gospel.

The court case closes. The Pharisees have found Jesus to be a sinner (v 24), presumably for breaking the Sabbath (v 14). They have expelled his follower the blind man (v 34). But suddenly we see that the story contains a case within a case. For the real judge appears — Jesus: and the Pharisees are the accused (vv 39- 41). So Jesus as the light of the world exposes their sin and their spiritual blindness and the falseness of their judgement. The representative of the new humanity (cf Daniel 7:13f) has come to judge the world.

Discussion

Jesus' conflict with the ruling authorities of his time reminded us that the antagonism of the state towards Christians is nothing new. Indeed if Christians are faithful to their Lord, this is inevitable. But often the propaganda of the state blinds people to the truth. They serve the state, believing that they are serving God. We discussed some of the ways in which Christians were obliged to choose between serving God and serving the state. Military conscription was one topic and the whole issue of nuclear weapons another. We finished by speaking about the cost of choosing to follow Christ.

Reflection

Gunfire erupted all around and he threw himself to the ground. For a few minutes the war blazed on about him, then it was over and just the smoke and the bodies remained. More dead terrorists, he thought. And watched as they emptied out the pockets of the enemy. Christianity against the Soviets, the greedy communists that came over the border to snatch freedom from the people of South Africa. That was the name of the game. That was what he had been taught at school, in church and now in the army. He looked at these so-called communists. Young men, like himself. What a pity they had not had the chance to become a Christian like he had. Then they would have been on the same side of the war.

'What's that?' he called as he saw a red book taken from one of the dead men. 'Nothing', said the white soldier, 'just a Bible. We often find them in their breast pockets. Once we even found a set of Scripture Union notes!'

Often when we sit in judgement we are actually on trial.

10. Equality in Service

John 13:1-14

As we entered into the last session in this series, we decided to focus upon practical areas of action. We realized that knowing the truth and acting upon it are often poles apart. Yet what other test of our faith is there, apart from our actions?

We started the session with a few short dramatic sketches on the theme of washing one another's feet. We enacted in pairs a variety of situations in which modern counterparts to that theme were acted out. So we had a family situation, a social situation involving a rich and a poor person, a black/white situation and others. You will obviously choose situations drawn from your own society. We were awakened to the ways in which we inflict hurt on others, as well as to some imaginative ways in which we can redress some of the hurt.

[1] **It was just before the Passover Feast. Jesus knew that the time had come for him to leave this world and go to the Father. Having loved his own who were in the world, he now showed them the full extent of his love.**

[2] **The evening meal was being served, and the devil had already prompted Judas Iscariot, son of Simon, to betray Jesus.**

[3] **Jesus knew that the Father had put all things under his power, and that he had come from God and was returning to God,**

[4] **so he got up from the meal, took off his outer clothing and wrapped a towel around his waist.**

[5] **After that, he poured water into a basin and began to wash his disciples' feet, drying them with the towel that was wrapped around him.**

[6] **He came to Simon Peter, who said to him, 'Lord, are you going to wash my feet?'**

[7] **Jesus replied, 'You do not realize now what I am doing, but later you will understand.'**

[8] **'No,' said Peter, 'you shall never wash my feet.'**
Jesus answered, 'Unless I wash you, you have no part with me.'

[9] **'Then, Lord,' Simon Peter replied, 'not just my feet but my hands and head as well!'**

[10] **Jesus answered, 'A person who has had a bath needs only to wash his feet; his whole body is clean. And you are clean, though not every one of you.'**

[11] **For he knew who was going to betray him, and that was why he said not every one was clean.**

[12] When he had finished washing their feet, he put on his clothes and returned to his place. 'Do you understand what I have done for you?' he asked them.

[13] 'You call me "Teacher" and "Lord", and rightly so, for that is what I am.

[14] Now that I, your Lord and Teacher, have washed your feet, you also should wash one another's feet.'

Notes on the text

Background

The judgement of Jesus is found not only in his rebukes of the Pharisees, but also in his handling of the disciples. Here judgement takes on a softer tone and resembles instead the patient discipline of a good teacher. At the Last Supper, Jesus performs an action which serves as the supreme example for Christians of all time. Here is a masterful critique of all human hierarchies, and the clearest call for social equality which we find in the New Testament.

One year after the Passover during which he fed the five thousand, Jesus prepares to die (13:1). The timing is not accidental, for Passover was the occasion when Israel remembered the liberation from Egypt. The death of Jesus will bring universal salvation and full liberation. John points out that the death of Jesus occurred at the very moment when the sacrificial lambs were slaughtered in the temple in readiness for the Passover meal (19:31). This timing is confirmed by the Jewish Talmud (a commentary on Jewish law from the time of Jesus and later).

As Jesus, the stranger from heaven, prepares to leave the earth to be re-united with God, he offers a final illustration of his love. This action will help the disciples as much as the communion meal to understand what Jesus' death means for them. It will also bring a new form of leadership into being.

John does not tell us who was present at the meal. We know that Judas, Peter and the beloved disciple are present, as are Thomas, Philip and the other Judas. However we may not assume that only the group of twelve were present, especially since v 2 states that the meal 'was served'. This immediately opens up the possibility that others, including women, were present.

V. Soha

Text

The writer tells us that the devil has gained control of Judas (v 2). The inner circle of Jesus' beloved friends has been breached by the enemy. Evil lurks within the walls of the upper room. However, lest the reader think that Jesus is threatened by this evil, the writer assures us that Jesus is Lord over 'all things' and coming from God, now is about to return to God (v 3). The comfort of these words (echoed in Jn 14:30 and 16:11) rings through the ages and serves to console all those communities who fear the power of evil about them. For in the presence of Jesus, who can feel afraid of evil? Wet-eyed and trembling we come to Jesus and find in the circle of his arms comfort in all the nightmares of our lives.

In v 4 we see the Lord of the heavens stripping himself of his glory and power to become a servant, as he moves among the disciples washing their feet (v 5). Since the disciples were reclining on mats with their feet tucked behind them, they perhaps did not recognize the servant who so tenderly washed their dirty feet. Thus the miracle of the Incarnation is acted out for them and the reader. (Cf Phil 2:5-11.)

Simon Peter is the only one who objects. Perhaps he was the first to notice the servant's identity. Or perhaps it was his turn to wash the others feet. Whatever the reason, Peter raises his protest first as a question (v 6) and then in v 8 with a blank refusal.

Jesus warns Peter that only later will he understand what Jesus is doing (v 7). The 'you' is singular and refers to Peter's own discovery of the meaning of Jesus' actions. There is a particular message here for those early Christians who elevated Peter to a superior position in the hierarchy of the Church, like the Peter party at Corinth (1 Cor 1:12). The reader, of course, stands in the 'later' times (v 7) and can see what Peter cannot see, namely the symbolism of the Incarnation.

The enigmatic words of Jesus in v 8, and the reference to 'washing' (another word for baptism) suggests that the ritual of Christian baptism is close at hand. The manner in which a person becomes part of the Christian community and so part of Christ is through baptism. But there is more here than a lesson on baptism, and as always John is careful to point beyond the sacraments to Jesus. Like the miracles they are signs of something far greater, namely Jesus.

Peter now changes his mind and wants to be washed completely (v 9), showing that he fails to understand the allusion to baptism. Here again is that misunderstanding motif which John so enjoys, in which spiritual realities and earthly realities are confused. (See the story of Nicodemus.) Jesus changes to the earthly level of Peter's remark (v 10), telling him he needs not a bath but a footwash, and so introduces another spiritual reference to being 'clean'. Baptism has made the disciples clean from their sins, but they are not all still clean (v 10). Judas has changed his allegiance.

Jesus returns to his place as host (v 12), just as he would return to God's side in heaven. He has clothed himself once more in the garments which mark him as the leader and teacher of the disciples. Now he proceeds to explain his action (vv 13-17). He is 'Lord' and 'Teacher', but he is also the one who has performed this most menial of tasks. In turn they are to follow suit. The 'you' is plural and includes the Johannine community and it includes us. We are all to be servants like our Servant Lord (v 15)!

Discussion

We focused our attention on the way in which the Church had lost sight of its calling to be a servant. We realized that the words of Jesus carry a sense of judgement upon our present hierarchies, especially within the Church. We spent most of the time speaking about ways in which we could live out the role of servants within our community. We realized that until we began to identify with ordinary people, by serving them, we could not claim to be representing Jesus. Together we planned one activity which we as a group could undertake. You may like to do the same. We realized that there was so much we could do, that at first we were paralysed into inactivity. But as we began to live out the message of the Incarnation, that message took on a completely new meaning for us.

Reflection

In the lofty isolation of the University lecture theatre, the debate on the role of the Church in the country today continued. One speaker advocated violent revolution, another passive resistance. One person spoke of reconciliation and another of dividing churches. That the kairos (moment of truth) had been reached, everyone was certain, but what God was saying to the churches sounded rather fuzzy.

'The third way', someone said. 'We must be a third option.' But we wondered whether there were more than two sides to a war. 'Passive resistance without political involvement', said another. But we decided that that was really passive uninvolvement.

The truth seemed to difficult to comprehend, even when it stared us in the face. The answers to the role of the Church lay oustide the room, in the lives of the people who were the Church, but who lived under the constant burden of oppression. The time had come for scholars to listen to their students, for preachers to listen to their congregations, and for the poor to evangelize the Church.

We concluded by speaking about the ways in which we could make possible the evangelization of the Church by the poor. We realized that teaching 'grass roots' communities to read the Bible contextually was one step in that direction.

Some Suggested Reading

The general literature on the Gospel of John is endless. However, those studies which take a sociological or contextual line are far fewer. The purpose of this note is to direct the reader to some of these studies, for further reading.

On the social history of the Gospel, the writings of two writers are particularly important. These are Raymond Brown, *The Community of the Beloved Disciple* (Paulist Press: New York, 1979) and J Louis Martyn, *History and Theology in the Fourth Gospel* (rev. ed. Abingdon: Nashville, 1979) and *The Gospel of John in Christian History* (Paulist Press: New York, 1979).

A very useful introduction to the Gospel itself is Robert Kysar, *John, the Maverick Gospel* (John Knox: Atlanta, 1976). On the Christology of John, one of the best books is Marinus de Jonge, *Jesus: Stranger from Heaven and Son of God* (Scholars Press: Missoula, 1977). The appreciation of John as a literary work may be found in R Alan Culpepper, *Anatomy of the Fourth Gospel* (Fortress: Philadelphia, 1983).

Among the commentaries, there are several which deserve the title of classic works. For the best analysis of John's presentation of Jesus, we recommend Rudolph Bultmann, *The Gospel of John* (Basil Blackwell: Oxford, 1971). For a solid exposition of the meaning of the Greek text, C Kingsley Barrett, *The Gospel according to St John* (2nd ed. Westminster: Philadelphia, 1978). Rudolph Schnackenburg, *The Gospel according to St John* (Vols I and II: Seabury: New York, 1980 and Vol III: Burns and Oates: London, 1982) brings a great depth of scholarship to the Gospel, as does Raymond Brown, *The Gospel according to John* (2 Vols Doubleday: New York, 1966 and 1970). The most recent contribution to this category of 'classics' is Ernst Haenchen, *John 1* and *John 2* in the Hermenia Series (Fortress: Philadelphia, 1984).

Some important articles are the following: D Moody Smith, 'The Presentation of Jesus in the Fourth Gospel' in *Interpretation* 31 (1977) pp 367-78; Wayne Meeks, 'The man from heaven in Johannine sectarianism' in *Journal of Biblical Literature* 91 (1972) pp 44-72. On the location of John's community in Alexandria, see William H Brownlee, 'Whence the Gospel according to John?' in *John and Qumran* edited by J H Charlesworth (G Chapman: London, 1972) pp 166-194. For another point of view see Raymond Brown, 'Johannine Ecclesiology — the community "origins"' in *Interpretation* 31 (1977) pp 379-393 and Paul S Minear, 'The audience of the Fourth Evangelist' in *Interpretation* 31 (1977) pp 339-354. On the community itself, see Robert Kysar, 'Community and Gospel: Vectors in Fourth Gospel Criticism' in *Interpretation 31* (1977) pp 355-66 and D Moody Smith, 'Johannine Christianity: some reflections on its character and delineation' in *New Testament Studies* 21 (1974/5) pp 222-248.